How To Be Hilarious and Quick-Witted in Daily Conversation

By Patrick King
Social Interaction and Conversation
Coach at
www.PatrickKingConsulting.com

Table of Contents

HOW TO BE HILARIOUS AND QUICK-WITTED IN DAILY CONVERSATION   **3**

TABLE OF CONTENTS   **5**

INTRODUCTION   **7**

CHAPTER 1. BREAKING IT DOWN; THE ANATOMY OF HUMOR   **13**

THE THREE HUMOR THEORIES   **13**
KNOW YOUR HUMOR STYLE   **19**
FINDING THE HUMOR IN EVERYDAY LIFE   **22**
CONSUME MORE COMEDY   **29**

CHAPTER 2. THE BASICS   **35**

PUNS AND DAD JOKES   **35**
WHAT FUNNY STORIES ARE MADE OF   **40**
FUNNY ANALOGIES   **46**
THE ART OF MISDIRECTION   **52**
BE ODDLY SPECIFIC   **58**

CHAPTER 3. HUMOR—IT'S A GAME   **69**

RAISING AROUSAL   **69**
EXAGGERATION—IT'S REALLY, REALLY, REALLY FUNNY   **74**
COMPARE AND CONTRAST   **80**
THE POWER OF SELF-DEPRECATION   **84**

CHAPTER 4. WALKING THE TIGHTROPE 93

TEASING—HOW TO DO IT AND HOW NOT TO DO IT 93
SCHADENFREUDE 98
ACKNOWLEDGING THE ELEPHANT IN THE ROOM 103
VIOLATE ME, BUT ONLY A LITTLE BIT—THE BALANCE
OF PAIN AND RELEASE 109
MISINTERPRETATIONS, EXCUSE ME? 115

CHAPTER 5. FUNNY=SEXY 123

REACTIONARY HUMOR 125
DIALING UP THE CHARM 130
CALLBACKS 138
CATCHPHRASES AND MAKING YOUR OWN INSIDE JOKE
142
TRY "ACT OUTS" 148

SUMMARY GUIDE 157

Introduction

One of my favorite pastimes has always been watching standup comedy.

Originally, it wasn't even for the laughs. I was interested because I had been trying to improve my own public speaking skills, and I wanted to study the presentation of the comedians. They were able to captivate audiences, charm them, and make them laugh. They were certainly doing something that ordinary business presenters and professors weren't!

So I wanted to learn their ways. I started by studying their posture, body language, gestures, and manner of pacing, but I only lasted about five minutes before I was completely distracted and engrossed by what was happening on stage.

And that's when it struck me—being funny on command and making people laugh for an hour straight is one of the most difficult tasks in the world. What you're really doing is evoking an emotion whenever you want, at will. In that way, it's a little like casting a spell. Movies and television shows spend millions trying to do that, and even the best of them don't get it right a lot of the time.

People cry at movies sometimes, but it's a thin line to cross over into being cheesy and lame. Jokes in movies often fall flat or get repetitive, and even horror movies need to work hard to eke out a genuine moment of terror from an audience that has seen it all before. What I'm saying is that conjuring emotions in people is not easy—and yet I was watching my standup idols do just that, and to crowds of hundreds or even thousands of people.

Impressive, right?

At first, I thought it was purely talent-based. I believed that some people were just funnier than others. If there's a bell curve, there are obviously outliers. Some of us can run a mile in under seven minutes with no sweat, and others need an inhaler to walk up a short flight of stairs. We all have different predispositions.

But it wasn't until I investigated a little further and started reading about the comedy and joke-writing process that I found that there were certain puns, premises, jokes, setups, and methods of delivery that were essentially *formulaic*. It's not magic at all. In fact, there are tried and trusted patterns, steps, and even rules that most comedians tend to follow—the more famous comedians have simply mastered these rules and have learned how to play with them on an almost instinctual level.

Let's take a quick example: you may have noticed that comedians tend to talk about airports, sex, gender differences, and race. That's because one of the rules that comedians follow is to make their jokes easily relatable and understandable; otherwise, only about ten percent of any given audience will be laughing. They know (from trial and error!) that they have to speak about universal human themes and struggles.

Now, there's no world in which I can claim to be a professional comedian, but by studying and breaking down exactly what the best comedians in the world do to make people cry with laughter, I've found that there are proven ways to be consistently funny in conversation—any conversation.

When you understand the patterns and basic principles behind the things that tend to make people laugh, you'll start to see jokes form in the moment on the fly. That's the best part—many of us feel like we struggle with normal conversation in general because it's so unpredictable. When something is unpredictable, it feels like we constantly have to adapt and think on our feet, and that's a scary proposition because it feels like it's only a matter of time before you slip up.

But in this book, I want to show you how to completely avoid this feeling. When you know how to work with those tried-and-true patterns, phrases, and principles, jokes will easily and immediately start to form in your head. You can say goodbye to the scariness of unpredictability.

Being a funnier conversationalist in everyday life is about your mindset and approach, but it's also about learning to see life through a lens of play and humor. It seems kind of obvious, but the process of becoming a funnier person isn't something to take too seriously! In fact, being the kind of person who is always ready to respond with hilarious one-liners and witty quips that have everyone giggling is about learning to see life in general as funnier, less serious, and more playful.

When someone asks you about their day, you could choose to answer literally, or you could make an observation about their jacket reminding you about Michael Jackson's jacket from the "Thriller" music video. It's not a cheesy "joke" exactly, but it's a way of being that is more creative, more fluid, and a whole lot more fun. And with this, combined with the strategies and principles I'm going to share in the chapters that follow, you can become the charismatic and entertaining speaker you've always wanted to be.

P.S. I'm going to be talking a lot about delivery, tactics, and how to be funny . . . but you'll be reading all this on a page devoid of most of those things that would make it funny. Breaking things down in a clinical way can strip the humor out, so keep this in mind and try to re-inject the delivery and tone of voice to bring them back to life. After all, visualization is the first step to action!

Chapter 1. Breaking it Down; The Anatomy of Humor

The Three Humor Theories

What makes things funny?

"Funny" is a bit like "sexy" or "cool." It's pretty hard to nail down a concise definition, but you absolutely know it when you see it. And you know when it's *not* there!

That said, humor is predictable enough for us to notice a few recurring themes. Think about it right now—what was the last thing that made you literally laugh out loud? If you think back, you can probably also imagine a time when you nearly fell over laughing at something that somebody else merely rolled their eyes at. Maybe you love watching those ultra-mean "insult comics" or celebrity roasts, but can't understand why anybody would laugh at someone slipping on ice. There is certainly a trend for which comedy videos go viral; this means there are just certain patterns that tickle our funny bones.

It goes without saying: there are different ways to be funny. Now, this isn't set in stone, but there are broadly three different theories that explain why something is funny.

Theory 1: Humor Relieves Psychological Tension

You know how people say tragedy and comedy sit really close to one another? So much humor rests on the release and relief of things in life we ordinarily think of as scary, unpleasant, or stressful. To laugh out loud is to let go of some pent-up psychological and nervous energy—or so the theory goes.

Let's say you turn up to the office one morning after a car accident and a colleague sees you and exclaims in surprise, "Oh no! And you've even got a black eye!" You could reply in a deadpan voice, "Shh, not so loud or everyone will want one!"

It's funny because it releases the tension of what could be quite a sad or uncomfortable moment. According to the theory, the funniness increases in proportion to the amount of nervous energy released. Picture a terrifying earthquake hitting and demolishing the inside of a house, leaving the occupants reeling in the few quiet seconds afterward. Now imagine someone making a tiny fart in that very moment. What makes it funny?

This theory also explains the humor in the "relief" people get from being brutally honest, relaxing their inhibitions, or saying the thing that everyone was thinking. In this case, the tension could arise from everyone strenuously following some social rule or nervously monitoring themselves. Breaking or bending those rules is like a reprieve that makes everyone feel good.

Theory 2: Superiority

A man slips on ice quite badly, then instantly stands up again and takes a bow before casually walking away. People might laugh at this because his little joke releases the tension of what might have been a serious and dangerous accident. But of course, there are some people who will be laughing not when the man gets up, but when he *falls* . . .

Pies in the face. People falling or failing. Jokes that make fun of someone else or their suffering. Every "yo momma's so fat" joke falls in this category, along with all those YouTube pranksters who rile up others for a laugh. Imagine an annoying kid is getting ready to fling a water balloon at you, even doing a little victory dance waving it around in front of you—right before the balloon explodes on *them*. We laugh at his shocked expression for one reason—it makes us feel better about ourselves. This isn't as unkind as it sounds. Mankind has been laughing since time immemorial at others' misfortune. Slapstick humor is funny because we unconsciously think, "Thank god that didn't happen to me!"

Theory 3: Surprise and Incongruity

One final theory says that we laugh at what we do simply because it's unexpected. We go along with our daily life and things are humdrum and predictable, and out of the blue something bizarre happens. This doesn't mean a ham sandwich has to fly through your office window one Tuesday afternoon (although that would probably be pretty funny) but merely that your perception and perspective do a sudden 180-degree turn.

"My grandfather died peacefully in his sleep. But the kids on his bus were screaming."

"I can't believe people don't eat the crusts! It's nutritious. It tastes great—in fact, I think it's the best part of the watermelon."

"I was raised as an only child. I gotta say, my siblings took it pretty hard."

"I just watched that new Chernobyl documentary. I'm actually from the area and grew up there in the eighties, and I was able to count at least eight historical inaccuracies on just one hand."

You can probably see how this shapes up in practice: you set up a situation where your audience is expecting something, only to surprise them with a twist that completely subverts that expectation.

In this book, we're going to be looking at tips, techniques, strategies, and principles that come from each of these theories—sometimes all of them at once.

How to use this in daily life: Start paying attention to all those things in your world that make you laugh. Notice what stands out to you as funny and then ask yourself, *what makes it so funny?*

Using the above three theories, try to see if you can identify which best explains the humor in what you've observed. There's no need to get all forensic and technical about it, but think of it as gradually developing a humor sense (not a sense of humor!) where you are tuning into the deeper level of what makes some things hilarious while others aren't. Gradually, you'll develop an inner intuition for how to use these theories yourself, but for now, simply see where you can observe them "in the wild." You'll develop a "style" of your own sooner or later, but it takes some keen observation to know what tickles you.

Know Your Humor Style

While there are definitely predictable patterns to what people find funny, that doesn't mean that every individual person has to be funny in the same way. After all, famous comedians wouldn't be able to capitalize on their unique voice unless people appreciated that difference. Humor can be very intellectual and "clever," it can be rude and raunchy, it can be goofy and silly, it can be physical and slapstick, or it can be cringe-inducing and awkward. But while comedians vary in the content they use, they also vary in the *way* they use humor.

You use humor in your own individual way too. If you can tap into your own unique style, you'll be far more comfortable and natural in yourself and able to make the most of your inbuilt humor. In 2003, Martin and colleagues published a paper in the *Journal of Research in Personality* and proposed their Humor Styles Questionnaire, outlining four main types:

Affiliative humor is when we use humor to make other people bond with us. This means fun banter between friends and relatable jokes.

Self-enhancing humor is used almost as a coping strategy and is commonly called being able to "laugh at yourself." This is humor that pokes fun at absurd or difficult situations in order to lighten the mood and make us (and everyone else) feel better.

Aggressive humor is what you might guess—teasing, sarcasm, playful criticism, and being a bit rude. Like affiliative humor, aggressive humor is also designed to get others to like us, it just uses a different approach.

Self-defeating humor is not unlike aggressive humor, but it's directed toward ourselves rather than toward others. Making fun of ourselves and self-deprecating can be extremely charming and funny when done right.

Importantly, all these types of humor have one purpose—to get others to like us. Be honest, isn't that why you're reading this book? Even if it's done through gentle teasing or playfully putting ourselves down, the end result is that humor binds us closer together, makes us feel better, and hopefully, makes others think better of *us*. Looking at it another way, we can tell when humor hasn't succeeded: it fails to win people over, or even worse, it makes others actively dislike us.

Do you identify with one type or another? There are no razor-sharp lines between these types. We list them only to get a better understanding of what humor is and how it works. What's important is that the *how* may change, but the *why* doesn't—we want to be funny because we want others to enjoy themselves and, as a side effect, like us.

How to use this in daily life: Think back to times in the past where you have made people laugh and see if you can identify any of the above four types. Which form of humor did you use primarily? Which kind of jokes and observations tended to get the most reaction from people? This gives you a clue about your own innate sense of humor and what you're naturally most geared toward. Another thing you can begin to look at is how the same joke can be told multiple ways. If you notice yourself making a joke, pause to see what "style" you've chosen, and then see if you can retell the same joke but in a different way. You can also take a pause and try to integrate the other humor styles into your repertoire to make sure that you're not just a one-note piano.

Finding the Humor in Everyday Life

Okay. Let's dive into the nuts and bolts. One surefire way to be a funnier person is to find funniness all around you. You get better at entertaining others when you yourself practice being entertained. See the humor in everyday life—there's plenty when you start looking, trust me!

There are two good reasons to start living life with more playfulness and humor.

1) You'll relax, get more comfortable with the funnier side of life. There's lots to appreciate in even a simple slice of life, and it's likely that you just aren't viewing things through that filter. So of course you won't be as funny. A pineapple is just a pineapple, but it can be so much more. Consequentially:

2) You'll identify loads of awesome and humorous observations to share with others, i.e. you'll be more relatable, and nothing is more impactful than speaking universal truths.

A primary aspect of humor (especially affiliative humor, discussed above) is being able to share your feelings with someone and find that you are both on the same page. You might have the same thoughts as they do about electric cars, or you both might hate the same types of yoga. Either way, humor is a strong emotion, and it creates a robust feeling of connection.

Being relatable in humor means finding commonalities that create real bonds. We live in a world filled with real and perceived social distances, and it's common to feel like you're drifting through many different social spaces completely alone. It's easy to feel alienated and disconnected. When a well-timed joke lands with someone else, we realize other people can relate to topics, situations, and issues like we do, and this sense of isolation or alienation disappears for a bit. That feels good. No matter who we are or how different our lives may be, we all laugh . . . and we often laugh at the same things.

Relatability taps into our innate human need to belong to something greater than us. Learn how to connect this way and people will automatically like you—and they'll like *themselves* more when being around you, which is pretty powerful.

Relatability is *hilarious* because of the shock involved in discovering that something you thought only you knew or had experienced is shared in a big way. The subject matter is not necessarily what's important. The humor lies in the fact that you and that person now share a perspective.

For example, everyone has experienced burning the roof of their mouth with hot pizza because they were being too greedy and impatient to wait for the pizza to cool off. If you were to bring this anecdote up, it's going to be funny because it's happened to other people in the past as well. The key here is to come up with an experience that is universally relatable.

Let's make a list of other things people hate.

- Breadcrumbs in jam or butter.
- That moment when you're walking toward someone but you're unsure of when to make eye contact.
- The awkward feeling when you say goodbye to someone and then proceed to walk in the same direction.

- Honking angrily at someone in your car and then pulling up next to them at a stoplight.
- When you start the chain reaction of a set of dominoes, but it stops halfway through.

These are inherently funny because everyone can relate to the feelings involved. There's an element of relief here. That isolation we mentioned? You offer relief from that isolation because you're offering people a way to agree and shout, "Hey, me too!" Not only will you succeed in stirring up that emotion, but people are more likely to feel that you "get them" and you understand them on a deeper level. Here's how to do it:

Step one: find something small that annoys you on a daily basis.

The smaller and more insignificant, the better.

You can't talk about a topic that's too big, like government corruption, because there are simply too many shades of gray and too many heavy opinions attached to it. Think instead of those small annoyances and pet peeves. Burning your mouth on hot pizza. Losing your keys. Or, you know, accidentally turning your phone's front camera on and being confronted with a vision of yourself looking like Jabba the hut (a little self-deprecation thrown in for good measure . . .)

Step two: exaggerate in a vivid way how much pain that small thing caused you.

For example, you could go on a big rant about how you're surprised *all three* of your chins have ever managed to fit on a Zoom call. Maybe the pizza was so hot it melted your face off, or maybe you were thinking about calling in sick to work because you spent entire geological eons looking for your keys, when they were on the hook where you usually keep them in the first place (we'll look at comedic exaggeration in another chapter).

Step three: connect the two.

You can say, "I really hate it when pizza burns the roof of my mouth. This pepperoni pizza was like taking a bite of delicious acid."

When you exaggerate, you draw parallels and an analogy to something that people can relate to. You come off as funny because you're referring to things they've experienced in an exaggerated and vivid way.

Here's another example: "Ikea furniture is like a puzzle that's missing twenty pieces at the beginning."

Step four: use it.

For example, "That driver was so rude. I hope he gets arrested. No, worse than that. I hope he goes home and burns the roof of his mouth on some, like, *really hot* pizza."

You have essentially prepared these funny, relatable jokes beforehand, and now you can pepper them into your speaking to be more colorful, witty, and funny at the appropriate time.

How to use this in daily life: The next time you're out taking a walk, put on your "comedy goggles" and start to see things around you through the eyes of a comedian. Look for relatable things in boring, day-to-day life. Imagine how a funny skit would play out in the coffee shop you're sitting in. Imagine that something unexpected and hilarious happens when that old lady with the beagle crosses the road. At this stage, you're not actively cracking jokes, but still in observation mode. You're simply getting used to being in a certain frame of mind.

Consume More Comedy

There's humor everywhere. It's there not just in the fun stuff, but in all those annoying things we have to deal with, too. On your commute, at work, at the shops, at school. (Woody Allen once said, "Some guy hit my fender the other day. I told him to be fruitful and multiply, just not in those exact words.")

Seek it out. Watching comedy is a great way to get a feel for all these tactics and approaches on the ground. Watch a range of comics with different materials and styles. If something looks really awesome to you, ask why. What made the joke land so well?

If you want to be funny, it's a good idea to study people who make their living being funny. These are the people who have spent years—sometimes decades—refining precisely those things that really reach into other people's worlds and make them laugh. Professional comedians can teach you volumes about delivery, finding openings, and playing with opportunities. You also get the chance to find a few humor role models. I get that not everyone is super loud and obnoxious—your style might be more subtle and deadpan. Can you find any comics out there who hit the nail on the head?

As of the time of writing this book, Sebastian Maniscalco is my favorite comedian. He's funny, but he also has well-defined personality traits. He's cranky, critical, observant, petty, easily annoyed, grumpy, and easily indignant.

Having that list of adjectives makes it pretty easy for me to simply ask, "What would Sebastian do in this situation?" or, "How might Sebastian respond here?"

You can start looking at situations based on their perspective. By simply assuming their perspective, you're more able to find the humor in certain topics that you used to think were so serious. You're able to step out of your mindset and into someone else's.

Humor is a point of view, and you are using another person's.

Suppose it is Halloween night, and you're wearing a vampire costume. It's pretty easy to imagine how you might play that role, right? Everyone knows what vampires say in certain situations. Having a comedic role model does the same for you and makes it easy when you run out of things to say, or your mind blanks. Somehow, it lowers the stakes a little.

You can step into their shoes and look at situations in a novel way, and at the very least, you can find more options in how to approach humorous situations. If I can imagine what Sebastian would say, then I won't have a blank mind or run out of things to say.

Don't worry about being phony or not true to yourself—think of your comedic role models more as a crutch or inspiration. I can't explain it, but sometimes, imitating your favorite comedians ends up making it *easier* to be yourself. You're just temporarily borrowing their confidence!

How to use this in daily life: You might also try consuming comedy you *dislike*. Ask why you didn't laugh. How could you change the content or delivery to make it funnier? First watch a clip as an audience member and simply note your immediate response. Then watch the clip again imagining you're a comedy expert, and try to analyze what you see. How would you improve things?

If you're not morally opposed, just give emulating them a shot. Go ahead, emulate one of their jokes out loud and see how it feels to intentionally try to be funny. It might be awkward at first, but after a while, you should have a good idea for what comes more naturally to you. Just don't judge yourself by the first run and give up completely when even your dog turns away from you in disappointment.

Takeaways:

- There are three main theories of humor, i.e. what makes things funny. The first is that humor is a release from psychological tension, the second is that humor allows us to feel a sense of superiority relative to others (who we're laughing at), and the third is that humor arises from a sense of surprise, novelty, or incongruence—on realizing an absurd or unexpected contrast, our reaction is to laugh. Humor can be a blend of all three!

- It's important to know your own humor style so you can work with it. Humor can be affiliative, aggressive, self-enhancing, or self-defeating—but in every case, it gets others to feel good and like you. This is the ultimate goal of being a funnier person.

- Funny people naturally find humor in everyday life. Humor succeeds when it's relatable, so look around your world for things that other people might relate to. Identify a minor annoyance or observation, then exaggerate it for comedic effect to create familiarity and closeness.

- You can develop your own sense of comedy by deliberately seeking out material from professional comedians, especially those you like the most.

Become curious about *why* something lands as funny, and see if you can replicate the same thing in your own life.

Chapter 2. The Basics

Puns and Dad Jokes

There's no one joke that is universally funny, right? Wrong! There is, and this is it:

Two hunters are in the forest when one of them stops breathing and passes out. The other hunter gets his phone and calls 911. "Help! My friend is dead! What should I do?" The operator tells him, "Okay, calm down. I'm here to help. First, let's make sure he's dead." There's a brief silence, and the operator hears a loud shot ringing out. The hunter comes back on the phone and says, "Okay, now what?"

Okay, okay, save your rotten tomatoes. Richard Wiseman (not "wise guy") is a humor researcher and has been interested in the ways that sex, age, nationality, and culture affect what we find funny. In his extensive humor research trying to understand the funniest jokes in the world, Wiseman found that shorter was better, and that jokes like the above scored highly.

Whether you like the above joke or not, you probably see that funniness is complex; it's not about the material but the way the listener's attitudes and perspectives make them see that material. Let's take a look at that classic and ancient art form, the noble dad joke. Don't know what a dad joke is? Here you go:

Q: What's brown and sticky?

A: A stick.

If you made an audible groan when reading that one, congratulations, you now understand what a dad joke is. Laughing out loud and cringing in embarrassment, it turns out, are close cousins. Loved and maligned in equal measure, dad jokes are usually based on cheesy puns and things that five-year-olds *might* find funny. Yet despite how corny they may be, there's something endearing and comforting about a good dad joke. Okay, despite the cover of this book, dad jokes are pretty solid in almost every situation.

When you're starting out on your mission to be funnier, a good place to start is with dad jokes (yes, really) since they're easy, low risk, gentle, and the least likely to offend. What can I say, people can't help but laugh, even when it's decidedly "anti-humor."

Q: "What did the farmer say when he couldn't find his tractor?"

A: "Where's my tractor?"

To get better at dad jokes, try spending more time around kids, who are experts at awful and unsophisticated wordplay (expect butt and poop jokes, also). You don't have to be clever or witty. You might think making a lame dad joke is embarrassing, but there's a secret charm to this kind of humor: it disarms people. It lets them know that you don't take yourself too seriously, and invites them to do the same.

There's a comfort and familiarity in that, and it instantly breaks down barriers and creates more intimacy. It's like taking a step away from all the stress and drama of life for a moment and going back to a simpler (and yes, slightly stupider) time.

This is important: sometimes, jokes don't even need to be funny to "work." Dad jokes are warm, cozy, and inclusive, and there's very little chance people won't "get" it. At the same time, you get to self-deprecate as others groan and roll their eyes . . . all while fostering a sense of closeness. Remember that the point of humor is usually to get people to like you? The humble dad joke is a heavy lifter in this area.

It's easy to get good at puns and wordplay. It's even easier to be slightly and hilariously *bad* at puns:

- Look for double meanings so you can be deliberately misunderstood. ("People are dying to get into that cemetery, you know," or, "Did you hear about the kidnapping at school? It's fine, he woke up eventually.")

- Look for simple words that sound the same. ("What do you call a pig that does karate? A pork chop.")
- Think about words that rhyme and put them together.
- Make up silly lyrics to well-known songs. ("Woah, we're halfway there, woah-oh, frilly underwear!")
- Purposefully mispronounce something to humorous effect.
- Try spoonerisms, where you deliberately mix up words or parts of words, e.g. saying "a bottle in front of me" instead of "a frontal lobotomy," or calling it a "bunny phone" instead of a funny bone.

Dad jokes are short, simple, and not at all about showcasing your wit or intelligence. You can mess up their delivery as much as you like, and they'll land pretty much the same: deadpan or triumphant. You can be sure to get people to give you a begrudging laugh. Love to hate them, or hate to love them, it's good to have a few dad jokes in your inventory. At the very least, you'll remind yourself that being funny is not rocket science.

How to use this in daily life: Dad jokes are easy. You just need to have the guts to be cheesy! That's the keyword here: *cheesy*. Try out a few with close friends and family first. Don't worry about being lame—that's kind of the point. Put on your comedy goggles again and look for opportunities. If you're feeling really analytical about it all, you could follow dedicated dad joke subreddits, join online forums or Twitter groups, or even buy some high-end literature like *101 Animal Crackers for Kids*. Forget about perfect delivery—you're just practicing saying corny one-liners with a straight face!

What Funny Stories are Made Of

Okay, okay, I get it. Dad jokes are great, but they only take you so far. When you pictured yourself being witty and dazzling, the vision probably didn't include you telling knock-knock jokes in the bar.

Let's expand our repertoire and take a look at how to tell funny stories. If you've ever tried to relate a humorous anecdote but completely fluffed the punchline, then you know how much of an art it is to tell a tale in just the right way. You don't have to be a professional comedian who finetunes their "tight five" for years before testing it on a crowd, though. But it is worth understanding the structure of a good story so you can prepare a little next time you have a good yarn to weave.

First things first: thoughtful, solemn, and wise are great—but they don't make people laugh, and they don't create that sense of relatability. You can actually talk more effectively about the Big Ideas if you're funny about it. It's all about finding that pop of identification and that feeling that the other person hears you and gets you.

Second thing: you need to practice. Yes, some people may *appear* like it's second nature to them, but believe me, they've worked at it. If you don't believe me, watch old clips of comedians before they were famous. It's awful, truly.

Finally, remember the two hunters in the forest? I'm sure you can imagine that story told in such a way as to make it seem really sad and tragic. That's because the emotional impact of a story isn't about the content, it's about the delivery. Any story can be a funny story. A funny story is simply any story told in a funny way, i.e. a joke. The comedy comes down to *how* that story is told.

Here's how you structure your story according to the classic three-part story arc. You don't start with the punchline, right? You get there slowly. You take your listeners on a mini journey. The intensity rises, peaks, then falls. According to the theories we've looked at, you build in a little surprise, you set up tension and release it, or maybe you have a good-natured laugh at someone else's expense—or all three.

Meet the characters: You introduce the people and their world. You outline their normal everyday life so you can put what's about to happen in context.

Introduce the tension: Along comes a need. Now there's a problem. Maybe a stranger comes to town.

The journey: The action rises, and your hero (is it you?) goes on a quest to battle the dragon, find the magic gem, or discover who stole his lunch from the office fridge.

Climax: This is the punchline, the outcome, the twist. How did the journey end?

Return: The hero returns from his journey a changed man. There are lessons learned. Lives are changed. Lunchtime will never be the same again.

You'll find some variation of the above in screenwriting workshops and literary how-to books, but the idea is the same—set the scene, introduce a new element, watch the drama unfold to a climax, then wrap things up. Forget any of these elements and your story won't feel as natural or psychologically satisfying. First step to telling funny stories, after all, is learning how to tell a story in general.

When you set the scene, you use relatability to build rapport and stoke interest. When you reach the climax, you introduce a sudden surprise or release some tension built up in the journey phase. Here's a funny story:

"I was walking my dog at the dog park the other day like always, and you know, it's pretty quiet in the afternoons. So there I am, waiting for Biscuit to do his business, and I start singing to myself, thinking nobody could hear me. I was really getting into it (yes, I admit it, I sing in the shower too, but that's another story) when this guy appears out of nowhere and smiles at me, saying, 'You know, I always used to wish I could sing.' I smiled back and puffed my chest a little bit. 'But now I just wish *you* could,' he said."

The characters are introduced and the scene is set (pretty relatable, right? Everyone has been caught singing to themselves—or at least they worry they will be!), and then the unexpected happens: a stranger appears. The speaker puffs their chest, but no! The joke is the sudden reversal of his fortunes, and we laugh at the misfortune and sudden deflation. This joke lacks a "return" section, but that's okay— we can imagine the stranger walking off and the speaker standing there, dumbfounded, while Biscuit finishes his business in the bushes. Sometimes, silence is the best way to tell part of a story!

The great thing about funny stories is that you can practice your delivery beforehand. Just like the pros do, experiment with different ways of delivering the same info. Make sure your story is complete, i.e. don't skip the important parts. You might like to have a few funny anecdotes lined up—those stories that you know get a laugh every time you tell them.

How to use this in daily life: This is something you can practice. Stand in front of a mirror, get relaxed, and practice telling the story of your favorite movie, paying attention to the narrative "beats" outlined above. Truly write them out and try to fit your anecdotes or observations into that structure. Keep it simple and dedicate just a sentence or two to each component. Pay attention to keeping your voice, facial expression, and gestures varied and interesting. At first, don't worry too much about making anything funny—you want to simply get comfortable with moving smoothly through a natural story arc with a good pace.

Funny Analogies

Are you familiar with the comedian John Oliver? Sole host of the comedy show *Last Week Tonight*, Oliver has earned a reputation for tackling the big issues in a novel way. He's especially well-known for a particular style of joke that he has really perfected and made his own: the analogy. Take a look.

"The poverty line is like the age of consent: if you find yourself parsing exactly where it is, you've probably already done something very, very wrong."

"Democracy is like a tambourine: not everyone can be trusted with it."

"The death penalty is like the McRib. When you can't have it, it seems so tantalizing, but when they bring it back, you think, *Wow, this is ethically wrong.*"

What makes these so funny? Oliver is comparing two things that normally don't go together: the age of consent and the poverty line. The Death penalty and the McRib. He's finding something funny that they both have in common. Consider it a more sophisticated wordplay of the dad joke variety. He's made some funny commentary on *both* issues in a way that feels fresh and unexpected, and yet instantly relatable—not bad for just one line!

Now, admittedly John Oliver has really flexed his muscles in this particular niche, and you don't have to follow his format exactly. But there's a lot we can learn from his style.

1) There's a lot of humor potential in bizarre juxtaposition (this is the theory that says that unexpected things are funny)
2) The more bizarre the analogy, the funnier it could be—Oliver often pairs controversial or emotive topics in sex and politics with ridiculous ones, like tambourines and McRibs. The bigger the contrast, the better and cleverer.

3) You can be funny and share risqué opinions on hot-button topics *at the same time*

How can you bring a bit of this into your own life? First of all, don't worry—you don't have to be like John Oliver who has professional writers compiling jokes for him weeks in advance.

The skeleton of this structure is easy: find topic A, find topic B, then find some unexpected connection between the two of them and bring it all together in one line. I'll be honest: truly hilarious comparisons do take time to create, but with practice, you can learn to make them up on the fly—they don't need to be side-splittingly funny for people to sit up and pay attention. Being "witty" is often just a matter of appearing to others to be a little surprising and a little playful. Playing around with everyday expectations is precisely what will create this expectation, whether it's hilariously funny or not. If you search hard enough, you can find a common thread in just about any two topics. Winnie the Pooh and taxicabs. Backpacks and old gym shorts. Teslas and spoons. Spoons and Madonna. Spoons and Cambodia. Spoons and Viagra. You get the idea.

One easy way to start playing with juxtaposition, however, is to use what's called the "comic triple." This technique draws its power from the fact that people have been conditioned in many ways to process information in groups of threes. It's everywhere. The Three Little Pigs. Newton's three laws of physics. Goldilocks and the Three Bears. The Holy Trinity. Subverting the brains' expectations with a comic triple can allow you to introduce some surprise in the same way that Oliver does with unexpected analogies. Behold:

"There are lies, damned lies, and statistics."

"Join the army, meet interesting people, kill them."

"I celebrated Thanksgiving in an old-fashioned way. I invited everyone in the neighborhood to my house, we had an enormous feast, and then I killed them and took their land."

"I like my men like I like my coffee. Strong, black, and able to keep me up all night."

When you make any type of list, you build an expectation. The comic triple then subverts this to humorous effect—think of it like a very quick story and a very quick rise and fall. In a list of three, you prime your listeners to expect one thing, then surprise them with a third that changes the rules, goes in the other direction, or comes out of left field.

It's easy to use this formula, and it works every single time.

Step 1: think of a topic or theme

Step 2: in that theme, list two expected items on the list

Step 3: list a third that doesn't belong on the list at all

Bonus points if the third item reveals a clever word play or a slight jab at the expectation itself.

Take a look: "I love everything about her. Her smile, her sense of style, and how she never has any clue where she wants to go for dinner." It's not laugh-out-loud funny, but it's cute and unexpected.

Using funny analogies and comparisons is simple once you start practicing—it's all about subverting expectations or catching people's attention with unusual combinations. As with any technique, start by preparing some material beforehand; in time, you'll be able to construct funny quips on your feet. Just remember that the humor is in the unexpectedness. Here's Ellen DeGeneres going one step further and playing with people's expectations of this format itself:

"I've always said, I like my coffee like I like my men . . . I don't drink coffee."

How to use this in daily life: You don't have to reinvent the wheel each time. You can make a joke by simply playing with the material surrounding you. Look for groups of three in your environment, then quickly subvert the expectation by replacing the third thing in the list with something outlandish. Let's say someone is heading to the store and asks if you need anything. You could quip, "Yes, please! I need some diet

Coke, cat food, and . . . oh, some arsenic, too, if you can get it." It's not a full-on joke, but it gets your humor muscles warmed up and makes room for follow-up banter.

The Art of Misdirection

When you play with people's ingrained expectations, you're letting assumptions do the heavy lifting for you. But you can always take a more active role and deliberately set up those conditions yourself, leading your listeners down the wrong path only to reveal the big trick or twist at the end. When you use misdirection, you're a bit like a magician purposely guiding your audience's attention to the wrong place—and then surprising them with that fact.

Here's an example from the comedian Bo Burnham:

"I believe in the Zodiac. Yes, I do. Uh, this is something a little bit morbidly ironic: My grandmother was a Cancer and she was actually killed by a giant crab."

This one is so unexpected that it might take you a while to "get" what's even happened. As you listen, you're expecting one thing—a joke about how his grandmother was a Cancer and yet also died of cancer. The audience is in a comedy show and are actually expecting this kind of wordplay. But like Ellen DeGeneres does in the above, Burnham subverts all this and goes in a completely different direction. However, it's only funny because he first *sets it up that way*, by announcing that he's about to tell you something ironic. Can you see how the joke wouldn't make sense unless he explicitly told you to expect an irony? He misdirects the audience to expect this, then delivers something else. He creates the tension, then releases it—but in an unexpected way.

Here's another example from comedian Jo Brand:

"It's hard sometimes because the house is a mess, the kids are screaming. In the end, my husband couldn't take it anymore and he stormed off to the pub. I said to him: 'What are you doing here? You're meant to be at home looking after the kids!"

The listener has the expectation of a long-suffering wife at home with a house full of screaming kids, while her no-good husband runs off to the pub. Of course, the joke is that the wife is already there. In this case, the misdirection is used to draw attention to big issues and societal stereotypes—comedians who take this approach can in this way be powerful social commentators without ever getting too serious.

Here's another Ellen DeGeneres joke:

"My grandmother started walking five miles a day when she was sixty. She's ninety-seven now, and we don't know where the hell she is."

You can see the misdirection, right?

To bring a little misdirection into your own life, you need to first practice seeing the common tropes, stereotypes, and cultural expectations all around you. The whole point is that these assumptions are invisible. Challenge yourself to go about your day and look for all the ways that life plays out in predictable ways . . . then start to internally imagine what they would look like if the complete opposite happened.

Let's say you're at the airport and notice the drug sniffer dogs and security checking through people's carry-on luggage. The expectation is that if they find something illegal, they'll confiscate it. But then it occurs to you that there are a few different ways to "take drugs." You come up with the one-line joke:

"I hate people who think it's clever to take drugs . . . like customs officials."

So, look around you. Be playful and creative about it. What is everyone unconsciously expecting in certain scenarios and conversations? At a wedding, everyone is expected to gush on and on about how beautiful the bride looks because she is presumably as dressed up and gorgeous as she'll ever be, and people are expected to be totally bowled over by her. It would be pretty funny, then, if you said, "Wow! So stunning. Really, I've never seen a more perfect vision of beauty. Absolutely gorgeous. The bride isn't looking too bad, either."

Once you notice all the expectations in your world, it'll start to seem natural to subvert them. Look at how this comic does it:

"Isaac Newton died a virgin." (The expectation here is that the joke will somehow make fun of virgins—a perennial topic)

"That means I have one up on humanity's greatest scientific genius." (The audience is now definitely expecting the comic to brag about not being a virgin, and therefore being better than Isaac Newton.)

"Because *I'm* not dead." (Expectation subverted—the comic totally is a virgin and has been leading his listeners down the wrong path.)

The above joke could only have stemmed from the comic's keen understanding of what people are expecting to hear when you tell a funny story about virgins. Similar jokes subvert the very same expectation—in a cartoon, someone dies and expects to be met in heaven by the mythical "seventy-two virgins." But the virgins are not what he expects—they're all nerdy overweight gamers wearing fedoras.

You can use misdirection in many ways beyond the verbal, however. You could "mislead" your audience by the very way you speak, dress, or behave, inviting them to play into expectations and stereotypes, only to shatter them. Remember, the heart of the humor is in the surprise—you could create this surprise simply by saying something shockingly vulgar in a very prim accent, or behaving in ways completely opposite to what people would expect, given the way you dress.

How to use this in daily life: Notice where you're naturally telling stories to people in ordinary life. At first, simply become aware of yourself playing into expectations. Then, internally imagine what it would look like to violate those expectations before literally speaking out to do so. For example, notice how you're telling your neighbor how happy your family has been since buying an enormous caravan. Wouldn't it be funny to weave a long story that suddenly ends with, "So now I spend every evening in the caravan alone and the family has never been happier."?

You might want to incorporate this practice into the rubric you have for comedic stories. "What will people think at the beginning of this story, and how can I change that?"

Be Oddly Specific

If there's a theme I hope that you've learned so far from this book, it's that to be funny, you don't always need to actively attempt to be a standup comedian. If you constantly try to crack jokes and set up punchlines, chances are that you're probably going to be more obnoxious than funny. People will see the effort and not the humor. There's a whole universe of funny out there, and very little of it comes down to punchlines and zingers.

Know what makes things funny, know what makes *you* funny in particular, and make an effort to go out and find the funniness in everyday life. Then, inject this into every conversation by playing with subverting expectations, poking fun, or creating tension—that you then release.

Funny people are funny all the time, not just when they're telling jokes or stories, and what makes them funny is their openness and willingness to be entertained themselves. It comes down to personality—people who are funny don't take life seriously. They're creative, fearless, quick, childlike, and a little bit naughty.

Keeping this in mind, let's consider those people who are not necessarily jokesters, but who simply have an aura of humor and playfulness around them. "Colorful" characters may dress outlandishly, or simply have a way with words. They may tell a positively hilarious story that has everyone enraptured simply because of the way they describe things. Instead of saying someone is stupid, they say they are a "nincompoop" (when last did you hear *that* word?) or "dumber than a bag of hammers." They don't say "he had a few teeth missing," they say, "he had teeth like a row of bombed houses, bless him." You get the idea.

You can be much funnier yourself by simply refusing to default to lazy, uninspired language and instead use some flavor. Don't go for boring and over-sanitized. Instead, pepper your stories with zingy details, funny words, or unexpected and creative phrases.

Someone who "dances funny" is barely a blip on our screen, but someone who "dances like a gorilla cooking an omelet" catches our attention immediately.

Usage #1

The first step is to destroy normal adjectives from your vocabulary and replace them with something that you have to think about. Other people often will not have actively thought about it, and it will be unexpected.

If you wanted to say that your weekend was "good," what might be better and more descriptive ways of doing that?

Good -> imaginative -> splendid -> like a big Bloody Mary -> better than using the bathroom after a long car ride -> almost as good as Christmas morning.

It's not difficult, but it's not easy to come up with on the fly, either. Whenever you come across a normal adjective, think of what other synonyms you might use. Your listeners will love you for it, I promise.

Usage #2

Another way to inject vivid and outlandish imagery into your daily speaking is to simply choose to describe observations, actions, and objects in an unconventional and creative way.

For example, Amy Schumer has a great example of this when she describes her sleeping positions. She *could* describe how she sleeps as "messy" or "weird." She could even go another level up and say she sleeps like an "unsalted pretzel."

The unsalted pretzel gives you a mental image, but she does even better.

She describes her sleeping position to be "as if she fell from the top of a building" or "in the shape of a swastika."

There's your instant mental image, which now has the added intelligent humor of combining two very different concepts (sleep and swastika, sleep and falling off a building).

Another example of this is from PJ O'Rourke, who described his experiences with local military in the Philippines, involving contact with a small policeman who amazed him.

He described the policeman as very intimidating and scary, but also very petite. His exact phrasing was, "He looked like an attack hamster."

Even if you're not trying to be funny, just the way you come up with analogies on how you contrast and compare different concepts can make for really funny descriptions.

How do you master the art of humorous descriptions? The first step is to attempt to disassociate from what you see and just focus on the elements and traits of what you see. For example, in the case of PJ

O'Rourke, you would set aside the fact that you were looking at a police officer and focus on the elements and traits of the police officer.

He was small, petite, scary, intimidating, powerful, fierce, authoritative, serious, severe, and elfin. What are two distinct concepts that would fit the descriptions above? Boom—attack hamster.

This type of humor really stretches your imagination and creativity. You're forced to brainstorm what the basic elements are related to and what they resemble in a physical level. You exercise your creativity and come across as smart, interesting, and switched on.

Usage #3

The final way to use better imagery is to use popular culture references to replace adjectives. The more widely known the reference is, the better the joke. However, there is a risk some people will completely miss the reference and not know what you're talking about. So, tread carefully and know your audience with this one!

Let's pick a well-known reference to use: the corruption of the Olympic Games. It's not something that people know details about, but it's something that people generally know exists. What traits would you assign to this reference? Corruption, unfairness, inequality, deviousness, sneakiness, and so on.

You can use the traits of the reference to describe things, such as "That cashier gave me a one-dollar bill back instead of a ten-dollar bill. Does he work for the Olympics or something?"

You're replacing the word "corrupt" with a popular culture reference—a much more descriptive, timely, and vivid way of speaking.

Let's use another well-known reference: the television show *Game of Thrones*. Use the traits of the television show to describe something—in this example, "addicting."

"This octopus pie is almost as addicting as watching *Game of Thrones*. It's amazing."

It only takes a little bit of effort to begin replacing the words and phrases in your vocabulary to sound like a completely new person. Be specific, be colorful, be unexpected. Deep inside every one of us is a funny little kid with some strange ideas—it's just a matter of consulting your inner weirdo!

How to use this in daily life: Take up creative writing. Seriously. Poets, playwrights, and authors use many of the same skills that comedians do since they play with language. There are now great apps and tools to introduce you to a new and interesting word every day, or challenge yourself to pick up the thesaurus and come up with a more interesting adjective than the usual. Look at funny traditional expressions or play with using archaic or outmoded language. Your granny probably has a few old-fashioned but hilarious phrases—steal hers! The point is that there are over one million words in the English language alone, so you really aren't taking advantage of a low-hanging piece of fruit.

Takeaways:

- The "dad joke" is a good way to start out. It's low stakes, harmless, and guaranteed to get a reaction. Dad jokes are made up of silly word plays, puns, rhymes, and mildly humorous (or groan-worthy) one liners. The shorter the better!
- To tell a funny story, you need to deliver it in a psychologically satisfying way. First introduce the characters and lay a baselines context, introduce a problem or a change, set them off on a "journey," describe a climax, then have them return. Most stories fail because there isn't enough context and background established.
- Funny analogies ala John Oliver are a great way to be creative and unexpected. You could think of a topic or theme, then think of two expected items on the list before throwing in a third, unexpected item that shatters expectations. Or you could play with contrast by comparing

two very different things that are nevertheless similar in a funny way.

- Misdirection is about deliberately leading your listeners down the wrong path so you can heighten the sense of surprise when you suddenly change tack.

- Finally, one way to start adding color to your stories is to be as specific as possible. Use unexpected and colorful vocabulary, imagery, and descriptions in place of boring and ordinary phrasing.

Chapter 3. Humor—It's a Game

Raising Arousal

Let's dig a bit deeper and look at some other common humor techniques that you might like to try once you've gotten a handle on the basics. Get your mind out of the gutter—this chapter is about *psychological* arousal and how to use it to make other people think you're the funniest thing since sliced bread.

A particularly goofy-sounding study published in 1968 in *The Journal of Personality and Social Psychology* showed some evidence for one of the theories we discussed earlier, namely the "relief" theory of humor. This research showed that increasing psychological arousal makes people think things are much funnier.

Participants nervously agreed to take a needle and extract blood from a large rat on the orders of the scientists in the study, only to discover that the rat was a plastic toy (Are you getting dad joke vibes from this setup? I am.). The results showed that those who were most anxious about injecting the rat were also the most amused by the discovery. From this, the researchers concluded that humor relied on raising and releasing arousal (what we called "tension" earlier).

Again, the joke seems to lie in violating expectations or norms, or else pairing up something quite grim with something patently absurd for comedic effect. The scientists called this "sudden release from strong affect." It's as though anxiety and surprise are converted into humor—the more anxiety, the bigger the surprise, and the greater the feeling of humor after that anxiety is released. In a nutshell, the scientist discovered the premise of literally every canned camera show ever.

So, what does this mean for you and your quest to become a more entertaining person for fun and profit? It means you have to play with your audience a little. It means you have to stoke the fire before putting it out. It's kind of ironic when you think about it—the comedian's job is to ultimately make people laugh and feel good, but the way she does so is often to make them a bit nervous first.

I'm sure you have a friend who does this: they call you aside and say in a very serious voice, "Look, it's time we had a chat. I've got something I've been meaning to say to you for a long time. Please, I think it's best if you sit down . . ." and just as you're sweating bullets wondering what's wrong, they stare at you wide-eyed and say in a somber tone, "I was thinking we should get burritos for lunch."

You can easily imagine punching this friend's arm, but chances are you're laughing as you do so—laughing from relief and the stupid contrast between the worst-case scenarios you had playing in your mind and, well, burritos.

Humor, then, is a game. You churn up some anxiety, some arousal, some expectation, some tension . . . and then you playfully let it all go again like a clown lets a full balloon go skidding around the room as it deflates. Of course, if you just ramp up arousal without releasing it, that's a different thing: that's called being a jerk. You don't want to be a jerk (that's a different book).

How do you know when you've crossed a line? Well, recall that the purpose of any humor is to make people feel good, and by extension, make them like you one way or another. So, clue number one that you've gone too far? People aren't enjoying it. If you're the only one laughing, it's not a joke and it's not funny.

We've seen that a big part of what makes things funny is that we get to laugh at other people's expense; in other words, making fun of others (or yourself) is not automatically a bad thing. However, recall the Jo Brand joke from above. The punchline works because there is a rather sexist and outdated assumption that the woman is always slaving at home with the kids. Jo Brand subverts this and gets the laughs. But take a look at this joke:

Q: Why are woman's feet smaller?

A: So they can stand closer to the kitchen sink.

Different feeling, right? If Jo Brand had told a joke where the usual sexist assumption wasn't turned on its head but merely *reinforced*, it wouldn't be nearly as funny. In fact, most people (probably women) would find it insulting and stupid. Comedians sometimes say the big difference between good clean fun and any of the "isms" is a question of "punching up" or "punching down."

Punching down is essentially making fun of people who are already abused or maligned in society, while punching up pokes fun at those who sit on top of the hierarchy. You already know that surprise is a big ingredient of humor. And really, what's *less* surprising than the same tired old sexist jokes?

How to use this in daily life: Your tone and volume of voice are powerful ways to communicate emotional intensity. To practice mastering your full range, choose a passage from a favorite book and read it aloud to a mirror. Notice how you come across. Then, read it again, this time injecting as much emotion as possible into the expressions, letting your voice rise and fall, changing inflection and tone, and opening your chest to speak loud and clear. Finally, read the piece once more and this time go over the top entirely. The third time round, it should feel easier and more natural to express emotions. You might like to do a little "warm up" like this before any social event—think of it like stretching your muscles before a jog.

Exaggeration—It's Really, Really, Really Funny

There's a theme here—humor emerges as a function of playing with expectations, arousal, and interest. Think about natural humor in everyday life—all those things that are funny all by themselves. You know, somebody slips and falls, something stupid happens, a crazy coincidence comes along and confuses everyone.

These things have in common a sense of reality behaving differently for a moment.

Intensity increases, our interest is piqued, and we're momentarily paying more attention. One way to work with this natural phenomenon is to artificially create this increase in intensity yourself. In other words, to exaggerate. Some comedians call this idea "false importance."

In a nutshell, with false importance, you take small and petty matters (the smaller and pettier the better) and react with inflated importance and emotion to them.

You defy expectations and create an incongruity in people's minds. They expect a small reaction to a petty issue, but they receive the polar opposite. It takes them by surprise and makes them laugh from the juxtaposition (I'm beginning to sound like a broken record here . . .).

With false importance, you also create a slight moment of intense tension. For a heartbeat, people aren't sure if you are serious about your outrage or whether you're kidding. They prick their ears and pay close attention. When it becomes obvious that you're kidding, it's like discovering the big scary lab rat is just a plastic joy—part of the laughter will be from grateful relief.

What are some ways that you can use the false importance tactic and make mountains out of molehills in a joking way?

False Importance #1

You can make a big deal out of something small happening or not happening. You can become extremely happy or extremely angry at something small happening or not happening.

"This is TAP WATER? Do you know who I am?"

"You have TEN pens there? You sicken me."

"Is your watch from Timex? I hate you."

"Is your watch from Timex? Gosh, stop showing off."

Other examples include calling yourself a big deal when you get a plastic toy with your drive-thru meal, or incredible rage that you only got one ketchup packet. You can become extremely happy or extremely angry based on something someone does or says.

"I can't believe you parked there. It's SO FAR." (When the parking spot is ten feet away from the front door.)

"You bought three pairs? This is the best day of my life!"

The delivery is important when you use the false importance tactic.

Do your best to sound serious. Stay in character. Don't use a sarcastic tone, and say it like you truly believe it. Then break character in some way, perhaps by giving a sly smile, so people know that you are indeed kidding. Express the emotion genuinely, then break!

False Importance #2

Another way to use false importance is to misconstrue something tiny to be a huge, exaggerated deal.

This isn't about emotions like the last iteration of this tactic. This is about consequences and rewards. Take an inconsequential act and assume that it will lead to riches and a privileged life or a downfall into homelessness.

For example, *"Yeah, we found parking five feet away from the front door. We're royalty tonight."*

"I got this watch on sale for ten bucks. When do we start filming my rap video?"

"Yes, I got fewer fries than you. That proves my theory that all women just hate me. Leave me alone!"

False Importance #3

You can impart false importance by using official terms for silly and small things.

When you use terms that are usually reserved for professional and managerial purposes in casual or inappropriate contexts, you create a pleasing defiance of expectation.

For example, using management buzzwords to describe a drinking contest, or analyzing a Disney movie using economics theories.

"Now, when she drinks that beer, she's going to rank in the top quartile of all alcoholics. I looked at my ALC-1 report and the probability is very likely."

"I'd love to work for that company! They believe in equality in a Jungle Book *sort of way."*

Finally, one simple way to bring more funny hyperbole to life is just to be a bit . . . over the top. Here's an example:

Exhibit A: Man slips on a banana peel.

Exhibit B: Man slips on a banana peel because he wasn't paying attention and was instead walking while writing a poem about slapstick humor in iambic pentameter, but then he dropped it and landed flat on his rear end, and the poem was at that moment picked up by a famous poetry publisher who just happened to be walking by, and they promptly said, "Actually, on second thought, this poem is not all that good," and then crumpled it and threw it back to the man . . . who failed to catch it because he had just slipped on the banana peel. Again.

How to use this in daily life: Again, start with merely observing. Notice the ordinary things you might say in daily life. Then, practice extending that sentiment to extreme, ridiculous proportions. Notice that you ask the guy at the pizza place to give you extra cheese. You could extend this to imagining asking for so much cheese that the extra needs to be delivered in a wheelbarrow. Or you could imagine you wanted so much extra cheese you were willing to sell your house and your firstborn child to afford it all. You might choose to verbalize these sentiments or simply observe them internally till you feel confident enough to say them out loud. It's about recognizing existing opportunities in everyday life.

Compare and Contrast

There is power in the contrast between banal versus important (like John Oliver showed us) and in the expected versus the unexpected. There is also power in comparisons and in creative and unusual combinations that have us doing double takes. And, we've also seen that one of the big theories of humor—superiority—rests on the comparison of one person with another.

"Compare and contrast" is a good way of thinking about introducing the unexpected into your conversations or ramping up that comedic tension and arousal. In fact, once you start looking for it, you can't help but see compare and contrast in basically every comedian's set.

Comedy legend Bill Burr had a routine where he compared himself to Arnold Schwarzenegger: "Anybody here think they could move to Austria, learn the language, become famous for working out, then be a movie star, then marry into their royalty, then hold public office? How many lifetimes would you need? I'm on my third attempt at Rosetta Stone Spanish!"

His audience loved it, and you can see why—there's a bit of a superiority feeling in his self-deprecation (more on that later), but he also paints a more vivid picture by mentioning the very specific "Rosetta Stone Spanish," somehow making his achievements seem all the more puny in comparison.

Amy Schumer uses comparisons this way: "I'm not shallow at all . . . like the guy I'm seeing right now isn't even good-looking. I'm serious. No one's ever like, "Who's that?" They're like, "What happened? Is he ill? Should we call someone?"

I'm sure you can picture her acting out the people's different reactions, right down to the facial expressions and tone of voice. The humor is in how starkly they contrast! In setting up this contrast, the joke writes itself, and people laugh because they instantly recognize what she is saying simply by holding the two contrasting ideas up next to each other.

It's easy to build in contrasts and comparisons into your own observations when trying to be funny. Pick a subject and draw out two contrasting poles: men versus women, old folks versus kids, flying in first class versus flying in economy, and so on. Then, just play with those ideas and see what pops up for you. Remember, there is no punchline so to speak—you are just holding these things up together and laughing at how different they are. The next time a friend comes round to visit, you could say, "I warn you, in my opinion, I'm basically Jamie Oliver in the kitchen, but sexier. Strangely, all my friends say I'm more like the Swedish Chef from *The Muppets.*"

How to use this in daily life: If you've never considered it before, try joining an improv class. Improv will teach you to work spontaneously with what's at hand and make those weird and wonderful connections and analogies. You could also challenge yourself to do these exercises on your own—look around and try to find funny ways to connect random elements of your environment. In what way are cactuses and old men similar? What about New Jersey and sunflowers? A Thai elephant and a pumpkin spice latte? Don't think about it too hard—just play around and see what emerges.

The Power of Self-Deprecation

"If robbers broke into my house and searched for money, I'd just laugh and search with them."

"I always learn something from the mistakes of people who took my advice."

"Am I *financially* wealthy? No. Do I have a lot of material possessions? No. But am I rich when it comes to love, happiness, and spiritual fulfilment? Also no." (Bonus points for playing with both the comic triple and subverting expectations.)

"I was such an ugly kid, when I played in the sandbox, the cat kept trying to cover me up."

Self-deprecation is the act of, well, making fun of yourself. Ever notice how often people say that the most attractive quality in a mate is their sense of humor? It's because humor tells us that a person is psychologically robust and flexible and doesn't take anything too seriously—including themselves.

A big ego is off-putting, but the irony is that putting yourself down can make you seem more likeable, less self-centered, and more trustworthy. Someone who is not only aware of their own faults but can poke fun at them is telling you that they possess both self-awareness and a playful irreverence about life—very attractive qualities!

Self-deprecation is a bit like salt: you only need a little to make a dish taste good. Too much and you ruin things. A good idea is to actually make self-deprecating jokes from a position of strength, not genuine distress. If you're constantly joking about mental health breakdowns, extreme poverty, family dysfunction and abuse, you'll only make people sad and uncomfortable. Instead, remember to be playful about it. Here's how:

1. Identify something about yourself that you already know is a flaw or weakness. Don't pick an area you're genuinely a little sore and uncomfortable about, and don't make

a self-deprecating joke intending to fish for compliments or assurances. Pick something you're only mildly bad at, or something you're not thrilled about but have come to accept. Better yet, pick something that you're actually quite confident about, or else something irrelevant to you

2. Gently make yourself the butt of your next joke, using any of the above techniques. Compare and contract works well (you're like the Swedish Chef in the kitchen), but so does misdirection (make your audience believe you're about to blow your own horn and then surprise them with a self-deprecating remark) or exaggeration (your knees are so ugly they make children cry).

3. Make it obvious that you are joking and release that tension quickly so that other people feel invited to laugh along with you rather than wonder if you're genuinely upset

Let's say you know you're getting older, but you've more or less come to accept the wrinkles, aching joints, and mysterious overnight ailments. You could remark to someone that you're having a mole scanned that day at the clinic, and when they express their concern, you quip, "Oh, don't worry, I'm getting to that age when looking in the mirror is like checking the news—I know there's always going to be some new developments I won't like!"

In this joke, you have something relatable (the awfulness of the news . . . and perhaps the awfulness of getting older, depending on your audience), a funny and unexpected analogy (watching the news versus getting older), and a relief of tension (you could have had a discussion about how scary moles are and how you hope you don't get skin cancer, but instead released all that and just laughed at the situation).

In a way, self-deprecation is also a twisted form of seeking superiority, that second theory of humor. It's funny to look at a bad situation or a moment of weakness or humiliation and instead turn it on its head, showing that you don't care because *you yourself* will make fun of the situation, and in that way, it doesn't sting quite as badly. It's empowering. And it makes other people feel like you're simultaneously humble and down-to-earth and yet still in quiet mastery of the situation.

Self-deprecation can be charming, but know when to use it:

- To defuse tension, if you've been genuinely criticized or attacked (Lady Aster said to Winston Churchill, "If you were my husband, I'd give you poison!" and he replied, "Lady, if you were my wife, I'd take it.")
- When you want to disclose sensitive or awkward information
- When you're actually in a position of superiority and power, but don't want to boast or draw attention to it ("I've won the award? Were the judges drunk?")

When not to use this kind of humor:

- When seriousness and solemnity is expected (your counselor won't appreciate if you make jokes in a group therapy session rather than just own up sincerely to your uncomfortable feelings)

- You are genuinely "low status" and have underperformed or embarrassed yourself somehow (making a joke about how useless you are in the office when everyone is already a little annoyed at your incompetence will just make them more annoyed . . . and make you look worse)

- If you merely say something bad about yourself, it's not a joke. It still needs to be funny, i.e. include some tension release, word play, funny juxtaposition or surprise ("I'm such a loser" versus "I heard self-deprecating humor is actually pretty difficult to do properly. Damn, turns out I can't even do *that* right!")

How to use this in daily life: The next time someone teases you or puts you down, accept it. It can be difficult to dream up a self-deprecating joke on the fly, but you can run with a cue set up by someone else. Laugh and agree with their criticism and then exaggerate it or use some irony. If someone makes a jab at the untidiness of your apartment, for example, laugh and say, "Guilty as charged. But one day, I'll be on that TV show *Hoarders* and you'll all be wanting my autograph, just wait and see!"

Takeaways:

- If humor is a function of releasing psychological tension (according to the first theory of humor), then you can make a game of deliberately raising that tension (arousal) so that you can release it again for comedic effect. The greater the tension to start off with, the funnier your audience will find the joke once that tension is released.

- Create confusion, tension, awkwardness, or uncertainty and then make it obvious that you are joking. Be careful that you are "punching up" and never "punching down" or making already-marginalized groups the butt of the joke.

- You can also play with arousal by using exaggeration. Show an over-the-top or disproportionate emotion to an everyday situation to increase intensity and create a sense of "false importance." Irony can serve the same function.

- Play with social norms and expectations by using contrasts and comparisons. The surprise of contrasting two very different things can be pretty funny.
- Self-deprecation is basically making yourself the butt of a joke. You still need to use some other technique for adding in humor, though, or else you're just being mean to yourself! Self-deprecation works best when it's actually from a position or relative power or confidence.

Chapter 4. Walking the Tightrope

Teasing—How to Do It and How NOT to Do It

And now we arrive at the idea that's probably been floating in the back of your mind for a while: just how nasty and unkind can a joke be before it's not funny? Where do you draw the line?

Teasing yourself with self-deprecating humor is one thing, but teasing someone else is quite another. So much of what we find funny in life comes down to norm violations or the disruption of expectations around polite behavior. But you could easily tip over and find yourself simply being a jerk.

It probably goes without saying that insults, "dark humor," and sarcasm take a little more practice and mastery than something like the dad joke. Don't try this kind of thing unless you're feeling confident in your approach, you know the people you're teasing well, and you understand the context properly.

Professional comedians know that the joke is in the reception—if your audience is feeling insulted, then it's not that they've failed to "get" the joke, but rather you've failed to deliver it properly. "Good teasing" makes the other person laugh and comes from a place of playfulness and friendliness. "Bad teasing" is not received as teasing but as an attack.

How do you tease someone without being hurtful?

Method 1: Use Irony

Here's the official definition from Dictionary.com just because it's something that people can struggle with nailing down: "the expression of one's meaning by using language that normally signifies the opposite, typically for humorous or emphatic effect."

Ironic humor is when something that is the exact opposite of what you might expect occurs, or when you say something but mean the exact opposite. Example:

"Ahem. I'm so sorry, did I start talking in the middle of your interruption?"

Ironic humor draws its power from contrasts. There is a contrast between literal truth and perceived truth. In many cases, ironic humor stems from frustration or disappointment, perhaps with someone else. "Ah, you've made me breakfast! Yum, burnt toast, what a special treat." Perhaps someone watches you trip and fall really badly, and as you're lying on the floor, they ask if you're okay and you say, "Okay? This is the best I've felt all day." You're making a joke based on contrast and surprise, but also poking fun at the ridiculousness of their question.

Method 2: Exaggeration

Express your criticism or teasing in such an over-the-top way that people can't possibly take it seriously. If someone misspells your name, you could make a big deal out of smiling broadly and announcing, "That's it. We're over. I have no choice now but to kill you. Do you want to be strangled or bludgeoned?" It's all in the tone. You can go both ways on this: positive words with negative tone, or negative words with positive tone. The joke lies in the juxtaposition. Ironic humor uses different elements that clash with each other to produce contrast and a sense of the unexpected.

Method 3: Use Funny Similes

A simile is a comparison between two things that are not similar at all except for one shared trait or descriptor. An ironic simile goes a bit further and makes a comparison to something that is the opposite of what you mean:

"I'm as likely to vote for you as I am to set up an appointment with a narcoleptic proctologist."

"You're as flexible as a brick."

Again, you're creating a funny and attention-grabbing contrast that pokes fun but in a humorous way.

Just like self-deprecation, simply insulting someone is not a joke—you need to build in some other element like surprise, relief, contrast, or misdirection. Avoid poking fun at people you don't really know well, and stick to making just one joke at someone's expense before stopping to gauge the reaction. Don't be the person who carries on when it's obvious nobody is enjoying it! When making fun of others, it's important to do it in a genuine spirit of fun and playfulness. Release tension quickly, either by your facial expression or body language. A good idea is to sneak a playful jab in amongst other sincere compliments.

"Jack's my best friend. Real generous guy. He'd give you the shirt off his back if you asked him. I mean, one look at Jack without his shirt on and you'd give it right back, but you know what I mean . . ."

How to use this in daily life: Try this on friends and family first. Make sure you're practicing with people who know not to take offense. Pick something that you know the other person is not genuinely insecure about, and then, instead of making a small joke, make a big one—in other words, insult them so ridiculously that nobody could possibly take it seriously. When your friend has a birthday, for example, jokingly ask if they need help crossing the road or if they'd like you to cut their meat for them now that they're as ancient as they are.

Schadenfreude

This fun-sounding German word basically translates to "the pleasure derived from someone else's misfortune." The best way to explain it is with the story of two hunters (no, not that story! The one's already dead, remember?).

There were two hunters out in the woods, and they came across a huge bear. The bear turned and looked at them. It looked like it was getting ready to pounce at the hunters. One of the hunters then quickly knelt and started putting on his running shoes. The other hunter looked in shock at the first hunter and said, "What are you doing? Do you think you are going to outrun this bear? It's impossible. This bear is going to lunge at us and kill both of us. You can't run that fast!"

The first hunter said, "Well, I only need to run faster than you."

We laugh at the poor idiot who's about to get munched by a bear. *Schadenfreude* is one hundred percent about superiority as we discussed earlier—it's that relief of knowing that the bad thing is not happening to us. Perhaps there's a bit of relatability in there too since we can imagine ourselves in that position, or actually have been before, and our reaction is a mix of recognition and a twisted kind of empathy.

"Cringe comedy" is a variation on this—we laugh at the awkward person in an uncomfortable or unfortunate situation. Sometimes, there's an element of "justice served"—have you seen the video where a bratty kid punches a road sign only to have the sign spin around and instantly whack him in the face? Instant karma, in other words. There's a guilty kind of satisfaction in watching people suffer from their own misfortunes. You know how it goes—someone is being a jerk and pointing out someone's bad grammar, but in their critique is a glaringly obvious grammar mistake.

The rules for *schadenfreude* are not that dissimilar from those for teasing and insults:

- Don't blatantly laugh at people whom you don't know well
- Don't use this kind of comedy when the tragedy is genuinely distressing for the people involved. "Read the room" and gauge whether your joke will release tension or just add to it!
- Laugh at fictional or hypothetical people, or, if you must, at people who aren't present
- Don't overuse this style or you'll come across as cruel and insensitive
- It's better to laugh at things that are short term and easy to recover from so there's no real harm done

Schadenfreude works best when used in very small doses and when a situation is so *unavoidably bad* that you have to laugh at it to release tension. A fool-proof approach is to combine *schadenfreude* with self-deprecation—build tension with a story that shows you being a smug idiot or deserving the impending disaster somehow, then release that tension by showing how everything went wrong for you in the end. People love a comeuppance story. And if you laugh at yourself, people will comfortably laugh at/with you too!

Another good tip is to only tease and mock those things that are really out of people's control, i.e. accidents and random misfortunes rather than their character and innate sense of value as a person. So, it's funnier to laugh at someone who drops their groceries in the road only to have a truck run over their bananas than it is to laugh at how bad they are at math. Keeping this in mind will prevent you from accidentally insulting someone, and make sure you're laughing at the random absurdity of life in general rather than the shortcomings of other people.

The best *schadenfreude*, in fact, happens naturally! The next time you're presented with an everyday tragedy or something going spectacularly wrong, see if it can be an opportunity to make a joke about the ridiculousness of it all. Make a self-deprecating joke to invite others to laugh a little at your misfortune, especially if there's a sense that you kind of deserve it:

"Hey! How did your skiing trip go?"

"Marvelous. Trip of a lifetime. I'm a natural, of course. I find it's all about being really Zen on the slopes; that's what separates the amateurs from the professionals, you know? Even though I'd never even seen snow before, from the moment I saw those glistening peaks, I just instinctively felt I was home and that I would soon master it all. So anyway, I've now got two broken feet and I've been banned for life from the ski resort…"

You could also use the *schadenfreude* principle to gently poke fun at someone else's misfortune. Just remember that it's best to make a joke about something accidental/random, short-lived, and in situations you're confident will bring relief to people involved rather than make things worse.

Adding a little exaggeration into the mix can poke fun at someone but in such a way as to lessen embarrassment rather than increase it. For example, your friend is a notoriously bad cook, so when he offers you a meal, you make a serious display of crossing yourself and saying a little prayer, perhaps even asking for a quiet moment for you to update your last will and testament.

How to use this in daily life: Your best bet is to encourage others to feel *schadenfreude* because of your foolishness. Think about minor disasters or little inconveniences in your day and think of funny ways to present them to others so they can laugh at your misfortune. The next time you are tempted to complain or express dissatisfaction, laugh at yourself instead. "Excuse me, did you give me the correct change? Not to be a nuisance, but this will ruin my retirement plans . . ."

Acknowledging the Elephant in the Room

An effective comedic technique is to acknowledge the elephant in the room, which is something people actively try to avoid mentioning or giving attention to. Yup, it comes down, again, to relief.

Sometimes it's an uncomfortable truth that people tiptoe around, and sometimes it's something relatively simple, like the fact that someone's new haircut is a nightmare. There are always inconvenient truths that most people know and are aware of but are walking on eggshells to avoid. When you acknowledge the elephant in the room, you end up releasing a lot of tension, even with the person who might be the butt of the joke.

Why? Because you say out loud what everybody is already thinking.

Everybody knows there is a problem or there is something weird or something off, but they are just too polite to say it. One way to acknowledge the elephant in the room is to do it in a sarcastic tone. This is what releases the tension.

For example, if you have a meeting in a sweltering room, you say something like,

"Thanks for coming everyone. Let me know if you want some hot chocolate to warm up. I know it's cold in here."

If you are waiting to order at a bar and the bartender is taking a long time, you can say to your friend something like, "I'm so glad the service here is so fast. It'll keep me from getting too drunk tonight!

Finally, "It's a good thing it's raining so hard. I really enjoy a good flood this time of year."

Acknowledging the elephant in the room is all about pointing out the obvious, but not in a judgmental or harsh way. Tension releases because now people don't have to pretend that the elephant isn't there anymore, but acknowledging it is no longer uncomfortable or weird because you've made it light-hearted. You'd be surprised how fast this can make people like you! Think of well-timed jokes in awkward situations as a public service.

How can you start bringing some of this into your daily life?

It starts with being observant. Just try to see what's in front of you—no expectations, no assumptions, nothing. Just notice how people feel and what's going on. So much comedy works because people shatter our unconsciously held assumptions. But you can also shatter our illusions right there in the moment. It's a little like an "emperor has no clothes" moment. Notice what is happening that people aren't saying out loud. Notice the efforts people might be making to skirt around an issue or be polite.

Next, find a way to bring this hidden thing to light by being blunt and direct. Honesty can be so refreshing! Calling out what is unspoken is a great way to gently push on social boundaries and expectations for comedic effect.

You can address the elephant by using exaggeration. For example, on a first date, you can just come right out and talk about the nervousness you feel by saying, "Blind dates are so exciting. My favorite part is where you both try to convince the other one you're not a psycho." You could use funny comparisons. For example, you could be at a kindergarten where several kids are having loud, screaming tantrums and say in a deadpan voice, "You know, that reminds me, I was thinking of getting tickets to the opera soon . . ."

Calling a spade a spade can be surprisingly funny—it's all about context. Calling it like it is can quickly break down barriers and create a sense of intimacy. Remembering that humor can be found in contrasts, you might find lots of potential funniness in the contrast between social norms and etiquette, and being blunt. For example, when a real estate agent is showing you around a potential home and says, "It's a lovely cozy place with so many gorgeous retro features," you could say with a cheeky smile, "Okay, got it. The carpets haven't been changed since the seventies."

Maybe you're reading the abstract for someone's dissertation on class history and crony capitalism in Croatia and you say wryly, "So, to cut a long story short, rich people suck?" Just like the little child in the story who is the only one brave enough to say out loud that the emperor is not wearing any clothes, this type of humor is best attempted with a childlike sense of honesty and directness.

It's not about being cynical or disrespectful, but about bringing in a refreshing, direct, and unexpected perspective on ordinary things. It's also best when you deliberately point out things that are already uncomfortable, but in acknowledging them, you'd bring some relief. It goes without saying that you'd best not talk about any elephants that people are very attached to!

How to use this in daily life: Practice running an internal narrative with yourself where you "translate" things you encounter in the external world into their *real* meaning. Watch a politician's speech and imagine what he'd say if injected with truth serum. Imagine subtitles running in real life over a first date that decode what the couple says into what they really mean. Imagine everything you see—adverts, work emails, news stories—without the sheen of etiquette or social norms laid over them. Not all of your observations will be appropriate to share . . . but some of them definitely will!

Violate Me, But Only a Little Bit—The Balance of Pain and Release

Few things are as funny as what we might call *crude* humor. It's one of the first principles that entertains us as infants and children, when bodily functions are at their most hilarious. But really, bodily functions never stop being funny throughout our lives. That's because they function on a principle called *benign moral violations*, which was proposed in a 2010 paper "Benign Violations: Making Immoral Behavior Funny" by Peter McGraw at the University of Colorado, Boulder.

Humor is mostly subjective, and we can see this to be partially true, as humor does not tend to translate across cultural lines. For instance, there are no comedy movies that have consistently struck gold in international box offices because humor is rooted in language and cultural and contextual norms. However, action and adventure movies routinely break box office records because there's no cultural translation required for an explosion or flying car.

We can see that humor is somewhat unreliable in how it translates across people, and you can't assume that just because you find something funny, other people will even smile. Understandably, this makes it difficult to be charming and likable because however funny one person might find you, you could very well be insulting and nonsensical to another.

However, according to McGraw, there is one approach to humor that is fairly universal and consistent. Regardless of whom you're with, the culture you're in, or the social context you find yourself in, you can always draw on the power of the *benign moral violation*.

Researchers asked participants about hypothetical situations that breached a widely recognized social norm, such as farting in public or spilling a drink all over your supervisor. The researchers only asked two questions:

1. Was the behavior *immoral or wrong* to some degree?

2. Was it funny?

Volunteers read pairs of situations—for example, one where the food company Jimmy Dean hired a rabbi as a spokesman for its new line of pork products, and one where Jimmy Dean hired a farmer as spokesman for its new line of pork products. The situation with a moral violation—having a rabbi promote pork—was both more likely to be seen as wrong and more likely to make the reader laugh.

The other part of the study tested whether benign appraisals of a moral violation made it funnier. For one experiment, participants read a scenario in which either a church or a credit union raffles off an SUV to attract new members. The participants were disgusted when the church attracted members with a raffle, but not the credit union. But whether they were amused by the church depended in part on whether they went to church themselves; non-churchgoers were more likely to think that was funny. The researchers think this is because the non-churchgoers are "not particularly committed to the sanctity of churches," says McGraw—so for them, the moral violation seems benign.

"We laugh when Moe hits Larry because we know that Larry's not really being hurt," says McGraw, referring to humorous slapstick. "It's a violation of social norms. You don't hit people, especially a friend. But it's okay because it's not real." He points out a recent example, an Internet video of a chainsmoking Indonesian toddler. "When I was first told about that, I laughed because it seems unreal—what parent would let their kids smoke cigarettes? The fact that the situation seemed unbelievable made it benign. Then when I saw the video of this kid smoking, it was no longer possible to laugh about it."

There was a very high correlation between the two—the more immoral the behavior, the funnier it was rated. But that was only up to a certain point.

If the behavior was deemed *too* immoral, then it quickly became unfunny and verged into either cruel or simply distasteful territory—for instance, someone who spilled a drink on their supervisor only to get fired for it because they also ruined thousands of dollars' worth of laptops that they were carrying at the time. It might be a sort of *wrongness*, but it's simply too consequential to laugh at.

Thus, the researchers coined the term *benign moral violation*—the act needs to be immoral but in a way that appears harmless or distant and has no negative repercussions. To be truly benign, the violation should be purely amusing, inoffensive, and psychologically distant, which means it doesn't appear real or tangible. An envelope needs to be pushed, but never can it go too far.

We can laugh at others, but not if they are *really* suffering. Another way to think of it is that we don't actually wish ill of others, but we rather enjoy seeing the vulnerability in others and perhaps enjoy taking them down a peg. It is a little bit reminiscent of the *pratfall effect*, where positive feelings result from objectively negative occurrences.

Other examples of benign moral violations include the following:

1. Someone falling over and their pants coming off in the process.
2. A ball hitting someone in the crotch.
3. Making a gaffe when meeting someone famous or important.
4. Your boss spilling water on his pants, making it look like he urinated in them.

These are all a bit crass and contain a bit of *wrongness* but are ultimately harmless because nothing is hurt besides people's sense of pride. At its heart, it is quite *clean* humor, so it doesn't turn anyone off. We can imagine both a conservative grandparent and a rebellious teenager laughing at it; it can belong in a violent blockbuster movie as comedic relief or in a child's movie also as comedic relief.

Overall, this study tells us that there is a thin line we must adhere to with humor. On the one hand, we shouldn't be too afraid of *going there* when talking to other people. What we might imagine to be inappropriate might actually be what spurs laughter and builds rapport. On the other hand, your moral violation can't be too great of a violation; otherwise, people will be supremely uncomfortable and even emotionally affected. It's quite a tightrope to walk.

The underlying point is it's not negative to talk about negative things. You can bring up negative topics, moral violations, or whatnot without turning your conversation sour. You might even be seen as hilarious. There's a line, but it might not be as thin as you think it is. Take a few risks and don't feel the need to filter yourself so much; you're missing out on potential goldmines for humor. And for what—to avoid judgment?

Misinterpretations, Excuse Me?

Some of the funniest situations I've seen in both movies and real life have come from simple misunderstandings.

Bob misunderstood what a proctologist did and scheduled four appointments, or Jenny misunderstood that the generic name for a painkiller was an analgesic and is not pronounced or administered the way she thought it was. Which one of those was from real life and which was from a movie? Well, both were from real life.

Those are instances of lightning caught in a bottle. Wouldn't it be great to create those moments when you want? You can take the lead instead of waiting for an opportunity to arise and essentially relying on luck.

Misunderstanding and misinterpretation are great sources of humor because you play with two sets of expectations and operate in the gray area between them. Generally, the thing being misconstrued is fairly mundane, and the other person is most likely expecting a dry reply to their statement. Instead, what they're offered is something they hadn't considered, which piques their curiosity and makes them appreciate your wit.

Sometimes you have to be intentional about setting up these misunderstandings yourself, and that is the Art of Misconstruing: misunderstanding people in an intentional manner to bring about a comical situation.

In other words, playing dumb or confused and taking an entirely different meaning from what someone has said on purpose. It's one of the easiest and quickest ways to bring the conversation to a playful nature and break the mold of small talk.

The misconstruing tactic requires you to stay in character for a split second while you do it. Strangely and counter-intuitively, this requires people to believe for a split second that you truly mean what you say. Otherwise, you convey mixed messages and your words don't match up with the rest of your non-verbal or verbal delivery.

After that split second has passed, it will become obvious through your words and your delivery that you are making a joke. A wide, mischievous smile is the best giveaway for banter.

Here's a simplified example of misconstruing: when someone says "I like cats," you might reply with, "To EAT?" Pair your words with a shocked look on your face and eyes wide open. That's the character you are trying to convey.

You've misconstrued the other person by not picking up on their context or intent. Imagine how a foreigner might interpret those words because of a weak grasp of the English language. Where does the conversation go from there?

They'll likely join the banter with you and agree, such as "Yeah, but only stray cats. The domesticated ones are too fat."

Here's another example of how one of my friends used intentional misconstruing in a conversation. One time during a camping trip, I was amazed at a peculiar insect that had landed on my leg and I exclaimed, "What is this? I've never seen anything like this before." My friend leaned in closer to inspect what I was examining, then declared, "Yeah, that's a leg." My other friends who witnessed the scenario then also started examining their hands, arms, and feet while acting amazed as they uttered, "Ooh, what is this? I've never seen anything like this, have you?"

My friends misconstrued my fascination with the unique insect on purpose and reacted as if I had declared sudden astonishment of my true subject's backdrop, i.e. a boring, regular leg.

Misconstruing is one of the most common ways of creating a humorous situation. It is the basis of many jokes because it's easy to take a situation and steer it in whatever direction you want. It allows you to initiate a joke within most social situations.

This technique is freeing and empowering! It doesn't get old, and it can go a long way in adding life to otherwise generic or boring conversations. The bottom line is that misconstruing subverts people's expectations. It breaks the pattern of the conversation and spices it up. If done properly, you shake people out of the generic pattern of the conversation and highlight your sense of humor.

Takeaways:

- While it's perfectly legitimate to laugh at another's expense, it's a fine line to walk. Teasing should always be done in a spirit of playfulness—if people aren't laughing, it's not funny. Use irony, exaggeration, and funny similes to playfully insult people; it's better to target small things than attack their character in a more serious way.

- *Schadenfreude* describes the humor that comes from relishing someone else's misfortune. It can be a powerful tactic to use in small doses. Use it with people you know well or hypothetical or imaginary people, and only laugh at things that are accidents or misfortunes rather than innate characteristics, as well as things that are relatively transient.

- Acknowledging the elephant in the room is a great way to create intimacy and familiarity. Notice what is going on that people feel unable to address directly and make a joke about it. It's important that this bluntness and candor genuinely release tension rather than increase it.

- "Benign" violations of social norms and expectations can be very funny, but tread carefully. You need to balance the pain and the relief equally.
- Deliberately misunderstanding someone or misconstruing the situation can be a funny and lighthearted way to poke fun.

Chapter 5. Funny=Sexy

I wouldn't be the first to say that trying to make other people laugh is not all that different from flirting with them. "Chemistry" has a lot in common with that buzzy feeling in social situations where people are laughing and having a good time. Being funny and being flirty and sexy have one thing in common: they're about *amusing* rather than *conversing*.

When you flirt or tell jokes, your goal is not to impart factually correct information. You're not trying to be right. In that sense, the content of what you're saying doesn't matter—it comes down to *how* you're saying it and how that makes other people feel.

The default conversation approach most people use is, of course, to discuss and converse. There's nothing wrong with that, and it can certainly lead to interesting revelations.

The problem is that it gets old quickly and makes things serious and dull. It's not the ideal way to build rapport since it can be a dry discussion of facts and news, which doesn't tell you anything about a person's personality, nor does it allow you to show your own off. It makes it hard to have those sparkling moments of connection and recognition.

People discuss current events with colleagues. But people amuse friends with personal stories. See the difference?

The difference in mindset should be to focus on being more playful, not taking people at face value, and not worrying about answering questions literally. Just because they asked about the weather doesn't mean that you are only allowed to talk about the weather.

How can you do this?

Imagine how you would react if you were five years old—*that* is the perfect start for playful conversation that can build rapport!

If someone asks you about the weather, what are the different ways you can reply? Imagine the question is *not* actually about seeking information. Look beyond the words and facts.

You can ask silly questions or respond in a creative, unexpected way. You might create outlandish hypotheticals or address the elephant in the room. You don't have to give people straight, exact answers. People are usually far more attracted to interesting and noteworthy answers. Your goal is simply to feel good around those people and, most importantly, make them feel good around you. Keep that objective in your mind as you engage, and you'll instantly be funnier.

Reactionary Humor

To keep in the spirit of amusing and not conversing, here's one easy and highly effective technique: just react. You don't have to proactively say or do anything. It's the way you react to something mundane or funny that makes *you* funny.

All we need to do to be funny is to simply react to the situation in front of us by tapping an inner reservoir of extreme reactions. That's the key here. For any comedic effect to happen, it has to be an extreme and exaggerated reaction; otherwise, there's too much ambiguity about what you actually think.

For example, if we see a homeless woman dancing to loud Michael Jackson music, you might look over slack-jawed to your friend with an astonished face and wide eyes. Take your normal reaction of confusion and shock to the extreme. That's an exaggerated reaction that can be funny because your reaction says, "What the heck is going on?" You're drawing attention to the big contrast between what you see and what is a more normal situation. It's not that the homeless woman dancing to Michael Jackson is inherently funny—it's your reaction.

Just like with *schadenfreude*, you can play off of naturally occurring situations and make them funny simply because you choose to enjoy them that way. Reactionary humor doesn't require language or certain information. All you need is something to react to that people can see in plain sight, and then you can convey an exaggerated emotion to draw attention to the absurd.

You contrast the situation you're in and your evaluation of it. As with the above example with the homeless woman dancing, the emotion you showcase is confusion and shock: that is the first and easiest way to react in a funny way.

One good example of reactionary humor is the character Jim in the British version of the television series *The Office*. Jim's boss, Michael Scott, is ridiculous and outlandish but recognizable. Jim isn't inherently funny, but what makes him funny is the way he reacts in shock and disbelief when he's faced with Michael's absurdities.

In many scenes from *The Office*, Jim simply looks at the camera as if shocked, and the audience laughs. He sets up the contrast between his inner monologue and the situation at hand.

This also works because when we see his reaction, we know it's exactly the reaction that *we* would have, too. It puts a face to our inner thoughts and is like exchanging a knowing glance. Instant relatability! In that split second, we have an *in* with the other person. We feel like we're on the same team somehow. That's comedic "chemistry."

So far, a lot of the techniques we've discussed are purely verbal. But a lot of the magic happens nonverbally, too. Use your facial expression and body language. Be as over the top as you like. Exaggeration is your friend here, but you can also use contrast or irony to great effect.

For example, you're in a mall with a friend and you both walk past a mannequin in a clothing store wearing a really frumpy and unfashionable dress in the window. You could stop and say, "Wow! Hubba hubba! Lord, have mercy, did it hurt when you fell from heaven, baby?" paired with a facial expression a little like the emoji with hearts for eyes. Here, your reaction is not just over the top, it's also ironic, and the contrast is funny (unless, of course, your friend instantly agrees that the dress is indeed hot stuff, at which point you shut your mouth and pretend you never made the "joke").

Maybe you're at the mall and you see the price tag on something you wanted to buy, and you stare at it with exaggerated bug eyes and pretend to have a heart attack. This is comedic gold—many comics don't even need punchlines for their jokes because their facial expression game is so strong! They take their expressions and reactions to cartoon-character levels, and it's funny as hell.

How do you bring reactionary humor into your daily life? Simple: be willing to be entertained. Then exaggerate that for the enjoyment of others.

When you're trying to be funnier, you can get stuck in the mindset that it's your job to amuse others and make them smile. But a more straightforward way to create that same buzz is to be amused *yourself.*

Take pleasure in situations and find the humor. Allow yourself to be moved by things happening in your environment. You switch from being someone deliberately trying to steer a situation (which can come across as desperate) to someone merely enjoying it and letting it unfold (which invites others to join in). Again, it's like flirting. What's sexier: when one person is deliberately trying to charm and seduce the other, or when two people are mutually enjoying a fun conversation together?

How to use this in daily life: For just a day, see how much you can communicate without using words. Express your feelings using only your facial expressions. See what happens to a conversation where you replace spoken words with a simple look or gesture. When people ask you a question or expect a reaction from you, try to give them a non-verbal one. While you're at it, see what different effects it has when you exaggerate those expressions. I once asked a friend how things were going with her new boyfriend. She said nothing, only proceeded to theatrically "faint" in her chair. Without saying a word, she had instantly made the conversation funnier, more intimate, and more relatable.

Dialing up the Charm

Have you ever noticed that some people seem to have witty, funny banter with everyone they meet?

It's not a coincidence. They're coming from a particular mindset to create that feeling whenever they want. It's easier than you think, but again, like most of the tactics here, you will be strengthening mental muscles that you probably haven't used much before.

One of the easy ways to inject humor in any kind of conversation is when you create a banter chain, which is a playful exchange that feels collaborative:

A: "That's a heck of a pantsuit you've got there."

B: "Thanks, I had trouble finding a skirt to fit over my powerful thighs."

A: "You're squatting about 250 pounds now, right?"

B: "Closer to 350 pounds. Dogs are afraid of me when I walk by."

A: "You could use them as a screen for a drive-in movie theater."

B: *"Did that last week. The double feature paid my rent this month. Did you know the design for those two skyscrapers downtown was inspired by my legs?"*

That's a banter chain. No one liners here—*both* parties play off each other. Conversational chemistry is about going with the flow rather than pitching up with some preconceived idea of what you'd like to present to other people.

It's funny not because of what you say in isolation, but how you play off the other person. If the other person catches on, then this gets funnier the further along in the sequence you get. The situation gets more absurd, but that's the part that's funny.

It quickly becomes apparent to everyone listening that something funny is happening, and they will want to contribute to the shared experience. A joke was initiated, and both people **stayed in the joke** for as long as they could.

When you say something and another person builds something on top of what you have said, you create an immediate bond. This creates an instant comfort amongst everybody participating. It's as if somebody is passing around a bottle and sharing a story. It feels good to everybody because they feel that they are part of something, and this can produce very funny situations.

This is essentially improv comedy, where you collaborate with the other person to build a scene, or conversation in this case. At the very least, you're going to have a solid inside joke to build upon for further interactions.

A banter chain has a few main elements and a few rules. Once you learn the mechanics, you're off to the races. First, you need to misconstrue something, exaggerate, or make a non-sequitur in some way to enter the banter chain. You need to make the first move, so to speak. What's important is that it's a non-serious statement that the other person is aware is a joke:

Thanks, I had trouble finding a skirt to fit over my powerful thighs.

You've initiated a joke (not *made* a joke), and it's an invitation for them to join the banter.

Second, you have to see if the other person will play ball with you. When you make a non-serious statement, they'll either make a comment on it or they will go back to the actual topic at hand. If they play ball, it looks like the statement, *You're squatting about 250 pounds now, right?* If not, it would return to the initial statement: *That's a heck of a pantsuit you've got there.*

If they play ball with you, congratulations! You're in a banter chain: they recognize what you're doing, they're playing along, and now you have to figure out how to play along back.

So, how do you do this? You build upon the direct response that they give you. You agree with them, and you add to it by *exaggerating and amplifying the sentiment.* That's what *Closer to 350 pounds. Dogs are afraid of me* does. It takes the main sentiment of large thighs and makes the stakes bigger every time.

The easiest way to continue the chain is to agree and amplify. You take what they say to be true, you agree, and then assume that the hyperbolic sentiment is true. If someone has big thighs, then to you, they have thighs that were the models for skyscrapers.

You can continue this ad nauseam until someone breaks, but at that point, you've probably built an hour's worth of rapport.

The banter chain can be very funny, but it depends on how it started and how it proceeds. Everyone involved makes the choice to either say, "Haha, yeah," or actually participate in the banter chain.

Here is another example:

Normal statement: *"Hey, I like the coloring of that cat."*

Misconstrued statement to enter the banter chain: *"So, you think that cat is pretty sexy, huh?"*

Playing ball: *"Yeah, I want to ask it out on a date. You think I have a chance?"*

Hitting the ball back by agreeing and amplifying: *"Totally. Where will you take it? Somewhere fancy?"*

More banter: *"Italian. Some wine, some cheese, maybe some place with seafood. Let's see where the night takes us. Cats are nocturnal, after all."*

The great thing about the banter chain is that it allows you to make fun of each other and highlight a little bit of your wit and intelligence. It's not just about exaggerating what the previous person said since anybody can do that. What makes you a good participant in a banter chain is when you make a statement that is not only reasonable but also funny because it is creative and also creates references. You're willingly dropping your guard and creating a light-hearted moment.

Don't try to do this by the seat of your pants the first time. A little bit of advanced preparation can go a long way. Practice exaggerating statements people say to you. How can you step it up in terms of absurdity and outlandishness? What are the extreme consequences of the people's statements? How many ways can you say that someone's thighs are huge without actually insulting them?

If someone said something, what is the silly, hyperbolic consequence of taking that beyond its logical conclusion?

It's also helpful to realize that much of the time, you will be making fun of yourself and exaggerating negatives about yourself in ridiculous ways. You have to let go of your ego. You might be insulted by things people say, but remember that banter is supposed to be light-hearted and fun. Allow yourself to be the target and exaggerate negatives about yourself. If it makes you feel better, you're going to be insulting yourself in absurd ways that can't possibly be true or hit *too* close to home.

With proper practice and the right approach, a banter chain can create some of the best conversations you'll ever have.

How to use this in daily life: Take a risk with people. Challenge yourself to instigate a banter chain at least once a day. Other people may not take you up on the offer, but offer anyway. You'll get more practice whether the chain takes or not. It may seem counterintuitive, but try getting a good chain going with someone you're not especially close with. You can't control how they respond, but you can get better at spotting openings and conversational opportunities. Start with a basic deliberate misunderstanding. Practice with shop attendants, wait staff, or people who are only momentarily in your orbit—the stakes are lower and everyone has an excuse to terminate the interaction eventually.

Callbacks

A callback is simple and gets a lot of laughs for relatively little effort: simply refer back to a joke you've already made. The humor lies in the mutual recognition of covering old territory, but usually in a way that amplifies or moderates the original joke— making it even funnier the second time around. Do you remember the gag about the two hunters made earlier on? Classic callback. This is basically how inside jokes are born (more on that in the next section).

Getting the callback ball rolling is easy:

1. Have your ears pricked for something funny or noteworthy.

Notice what people have already laughed at, for example.
2. Remember it . . . have patience and store it away for later
3. In another completely different context, you spot a way that you could bring it up again . . . so you make the same joke again, or present the old joke but slightly modified
4. Sit back and relax as people laugh

Callbacks are easy, they work, and they're low stakes. They're the perfect tool for creating a warm sense of familiarity and can also help you get banter chains going—you could think of callbacks as drawn-out banter chains. Some good friends can keep this sort of thing going for *years*.

The only catch is to make sure you're bringing in the callback in a way that makes at least some logical sense. It has to be connected some way to the present moment. Let's imagine you and a friend had the banter exchange above, where joked about taking that good-looking cat out to a seafood restaurant. Let's say that one day, you see a beautiful-looking cat on

TV. You could nonchalantly say, "Wow. Now *there's* a cat that's definitely out of my league."

As you can see, it's not really a joke on its own. It's simply the same thread from before, slightly reworked. But it will get a laugh. With a bit of luck, you and your friend will now have an inside joke for life, and you can expect it to be volleyed back to you at some point in the future.

For those readers who are familiar with the show *Family Guy*, you'll know that once in a while, a giant chicken will enter the scene and have a massive fight with Peter. There's no reason for the chicken to be there, and every time it appears, the rest of the plot has to pause until the fight is over. The chicken does the same thing every time, but it's the fact that it keeps returning that's funny. It's the same thing in the show *South Park* where the character Kenny is killed over and over again. Kenny dying becomes a kind of shared shorthand, and fans of the show get a little thrill every time it happens.

Callbacks are easy and effective, but there are a few situations where they can be done incorrectly. Usually, this happens at step one in the list above. You can't make a callback joke out of just anything—the material needs to have registered as funny, noteworthy, or interesting the first time round. In other words, if you call back to a joke that nobody found funny initially, it's going to be even *less* funny when you repeat it. Make sure that the callback is at least memorable—you could even return to a joke that people found cringeworthy.

Callbacks can fail if there isn't enough time between the original and the callback. Be patient! Allow your audience to completely forget about it for maximum surprise when you reintroduce it. Change the topic, or if you can, wait a good few days. The more unexpected, the funnier it will be.

Avoid callbacks in an audience where some people weren't there for the original joke so you avoid alienating them. Avoid callbacks if you notice people genuinely not enjoying them. Finally, it's best to avoid cultural references as callbacks. You can never be sure that people have watched the same movies, etc. as you have, or if they have, what their reaction to it was. Sometimes, callbacks do expire eventually—even the "They killed Kenny!" joke was eventually dropped by *South Park* since it had been done, if you'll forgive the pun, to death.

How to use this in daily life: As you converse with someone, scan closely and notice what they laugh or smile at, or what temporarily animates them. It can be something tiny. At first, choose something *they* say or dwell on, rather than making a callback to your own material. It doesn't even need to be funny, really. For example, somebody mentions in conversation that they're allergic to peanuts and almost died once. A few days later, they ask you about a movie you saw over the weekend and you say, "Let's just say it had the same effect on me as peanuts have on you." Take note of notable things and then play them back to your conversation partner.

Catchphrases and Making Your Own Inside Joke

Inside jokes and catchphrases go hand in hand. Catchphrases are like in-jokes and callbacks that have been used so often that they have essentially become stripped down to just a few words or a single phrase that nevertheless encapsulates something funny. You probably already know a million catchphrases:

"Aaaaaaaaalrighty, then!"

"Aye carumba"

"Is it cos I is black?"

"Did I do that?"

"How *you* doin'?"

"That's what she said."

"Wubba Lubba Dub-Dub!"

Now, depending on your age, nationality, and TV tastes, you may recognize some of the above but have no idea about the others. This is precisely why it can be tricky to use catchphrases from pop culture—if the other person has no idea what you're talking about, you create the opposite of that feeling of familiarity and intimacy. You become that annoying person who seems to think that reciting jokes from his favorite TV show somehow makes him funny whether other people have seen the show or not!

It's far better to make your own brand-spanking-new catchphrase. The process is similar to how you start a banter chain or catch a little nugget of material to be used later for a callback joke. Listen carefully for a funny moment or a phrase that seems especially silly or noteworthy in the moment.

For example, in my family, there is an old anecdote about a time me and my siblings were driving in the car with my mother. A driver raced through an intersection when the light was green for her, nearly killing us all in the process. My mother was so furious that for a second, it was like she couldn't even find the words to speak. Knowing she couldn't swear in the car with the kids present, she kind of spluttered and stumbled for a second before saying in a totally outraged whisper, "You . . . you *criminal*."

It was hilarious at the time because of the juxtaposition of my mother's palpable rage and the fairly weak and unusual "insult" she chose at that moment. From that point on, however, the phrase "you criminal," said with as much hatred and disgust in the voice as possible, became a kind of catchphrase for the family. It was used in a variety of funny situations. If someone stole a French fry off another person's plate? "You criminal." That supremely unhelpful bureaucrat you just spoke to on the phone? "What a complete and utter . . . criminal." In effect, this word became a shorthand for all those times when someone behaved so deplorably there wasn't even a word for it. On the other hand, it was also used to exaggerate a pretty innocent "crime" and blow it out of proportion for comedic effect.

The best catchphrases are made by consensus. This means that if you try to make something *you've* said a catchphrase, it's not likely to stick and may even come across as lame (in fact, the catchphrase "Wubba Lubba Dub-Dub!" makes fun of this very notion; it's from the TV show *Rick and Morty*, and the joke here is that Rick is trying to get his own catchphrase started . . . and it simply doesn't work. In a later episode, another character reveals that this phrase actually means "Help, I am in great pain," creating a kind of callback within a callback).

Instead, you can get a catchphrase going by noticing what *other* people say and then referring back to it in another related context. Avoid anything that actively mocks someone else or makes them feel uncomfortable. Pick something that's amusing and sticks out in the moment. The shorter, the better. Listen up for weird turns of phrase, strange vocabulary, or odd ways that people have of pronouncing things. You could pair a catchphrase with a particular expression or gesture to nail it down. Hear it, remember it, then scan for situations when you could whip it out for maximum effect.

Which situations work best? You'll have to practice a little to get a feel for the best time to spring your catchphrase, especially if it's not established yet. As with all callbacks, give it time and don't try to force it. Then make it really obvious so that people can tell you've made a joke. Let it rest before bringing it up again. Take your cue from others—if they laugh, or better yet, if they use the catchphrase themselves later, consider it a success.

Some catchphrases draw their power deliberately from whatever comes before them—for example, the phrase "that's what she said." The UK version is "said the actress to the bishop" and is funniest when said after an innocent and unrelated phrase to immediately create a sexual innuendo or double entendre:

"I think it's stuck."

". . . said the actress to the bishop."

Finding just the right place to jump in with a catchphrase takes practice. It's hard, so take it slowly (that's what she said).

How to use this in daily life: Again, it starts with listening, paying attention, and noticing details. Be patient. Unlike most comedic techniques, this is about *other people* and how they share information. Don't force anything. Listen for what is unusual, what is repeated, or what is said with extreme emotion. Your job is to notice and bring attention to these things rather than create them from scratch. One surefire technique? Listen to what kids say. Maybe your baby cousin says, "foot fingers" one day instead of toes and you grab hold of it and insist on calling them foot fingers from then on!

Try "Act Outs"

Finally, one way to bring more playfulness, flirtation, and fun into interactions (i.e. how to get out of *conversing* and into *amusing*) is to forget about words and lean into the power of expression, body language, gesture, and nonverbal communication. This is powerful, primal territory. Little kids are experts at this and happily engage in pretend play, changing their tone of voice, gesture, and movements to roleplay different people, or physically acting out a narrative rather than simply relying on words to express everything.

In comedy, acting out is essentially telling a story, but using your physical presence and action to convey your meaning. You probably already do this without thinking about it, but the best storytellers have learned to master this ability to really bring a funny story to life. Acting out doesn't have to be dramatic or slapstick, however. Here are some everyday examples that you might not usually associate with "acting":

- When you relate a conversation between two other people, you can repeat their conversation as it happened (i.e. without saying, "he said, she said") using different voices and accents to signify a switch in role
- You could indicate a switch in role simply with a subtle turn of your head, or by facing a different direction to indicate the person's position in the conversation. You could mimic the action each person was doing at the time, or have fun portraying their facial expressions and gestures
- Use a particular gesture as you would a catchphrase—identify a single funny or noteworthy action that signifies something else and use it almost as a code during the story. Impersonators often do this—they zoom in on just one or two features when mimicking someone and exaggerate that

- Use reactions—yours and the people in the story you're telling—and rely more on implied meaning than explicitly saying something out loud
- Bill Burr has a few routines where he momentarily takes on the persona of a character in his story, then relates the narrative from that perspective entirely, leaving the audience to infer the rest
- Use movies and TV as inspiration. When you're telling a funny story, literally imagine that you're trying to convey cut scenes, different angles, and a variety of different characters to your audience. Watch one-man-show actors to get a feel for how to do this yourself

Comedic act outs are perhaps the most advanced technique in this book and take a long time to master. In fact, even the pros need to work hard to fine-tune standup routines that include this element. When done well, it's essentially invisible. The audience is so immersed in the story being told, they don't really realize that it *is* being told. When done incorrectly, it can come across as forced or confusing.

Rehearsed act outs are best left to the professionals who intend to deliver it all in front of a mic to a seated audience. But you can use some of the principles of acting out to make your stories livelier and more compelling. Start small and subtle before working your way up. You can convey a lot and get the laughs by simply including different voices, gestures, and exaggerated facial expressions. Leave the extreme pantomime and slapstick for when you feel more confident!

That said, act outs may suit some types of humor and some people a lot better than others. If your style is more dry and deadpan, and you find act outs uncomfortable, then don't feel you have to include them. Other people, however, may naturally gravitate toward this—these are the people who are good at impressions and always seem to use their hands when they're speaking.

Whatever you decide, it's not too difficult to build in a little physicality and dynamism into your storytelling:

- Be aware of what your body is doing in space. Take note of your posture and practice changing it up to help better convey your message. If you're telling a funny story of that time you fell out of your girlfriend's dorm window, change up your posture to indicate how you snuck around at night, how you fell, how you grimaced in pain . . . Your body has its own language; why not use it?
- Think about tone of voice, volume of voice, and accent. You can play around with contrast this way (by juxtaposing your words with your voice) or you can take a feature of your voice and exaggerate it (for example, using an over-the-top posh accent to convey the way the snooty waiter spoke to you yesterday).
- Tell a story with your whole body. Your face, your gestures, and your hand movements all have the power to say something. You can practice in small ways at first. Eventually, you may find yourself telling a joke with only a gesture (remember the guy who slipped and fell and then immediately stood up and took a bow?)

Acting out is something that's better done either a) when you're a professional and are happy to put in the hours to hone your story and potentially bomb a few times before getting it right or b) you're willing to let it emerge spontaneously in natural conversation and see it as primarily play.

One final tip for introducing act outs into your interactions is to notice where you tend to do it already, then ramp that up. You might notice you're good at mocking people's voices, or that you have a very funny and expressive face. Play up on those strengths and work with your inbuilt intuitions—a little goes a long way!

How to use this in daily life: Watch cartoons. Sounds kind of obvious but watching how over the top and physical a lot of the humor is will help you fine-tune your own sense for acted-out comedy. Watch old Charlie Chaplin films or slapstick comedies where the gag is all in the funny voice, the outfit, or the stupid action. As you did before, practice telling a favorite story in the mirror, but this time, try telling about ten or twenty percent of the story using your facial expressions, actions, and gestures alone.

Takeaways:

- Good comedy has a lot in common with flirting. To be funnier, keep in mind that humor is a collaborative, emergent, shared phenomenon that you can't control too closely.

- Reactionary humor is an easy and effective way to get the laughs—simply exaggerate and amplify your response to something in the environment, perhaps even playing with contrast or irony.

- Invite others to join you in "banter chains" so you can create a great flow together. It's all about listening for "ins" and then changing the conversation course by introducing something exaggerated, strange, or unexpected . . . then seeing if the other person takes the bait.

- Callbacks are essentially references to previous jokes, but only work when the original joke was interesting or funny. Be patient and wait for your listeners to truly forget about it before reintroducing it.

- Catchphrases are like callbacks. Avoid cultural references and stick to making catchphrases of things *other* people have said.
- Finally, act outs are a way to bring life and dynamism to your storytelling. Use voice, gesture, expression, and nonverbal communication to convey your story with color and humor.

Summary Guide

CHAPTER 1. BREAKING IT DOWN; THE ANATOMY OF HUMOR

- There are three main theories of humor, i.e. what makes things funny. The first is that humor is a release from psychological tension, the second is that humor allows us to feel a sense of superiority relative to others (who we're laughing at), and the third is that humor arises from a sense of surprise, novelty, or incongruence—on realizing an absurd or unexpected contrast, our reaction is to laugh. Humor can be a blend of all three!
- It's important to know your own humor style so you can work with it. Humor can be affiliative, aggressive, self-enhancing, or self-defeating—but in every case, it gets others to feel good and like you.

This is the ultimate goal of being a funnier person.

- Funny people naturally find humor in everyday life. Humor succeeds when it's relatable, so look around your world for things that other people might relate to. Identify a minor annoyance or observation, then exaggerate it for comedic effect to create familiarity and closeness.

- You can develop your own sense of comedy by deliberately seeking out material from professional comedians, especially those you like the most. Become curious about *why* something lands as funny, and see if you can replicate the same thing in your own life.

CHAPTER 2. THE BASICS

- The "dad joke" is a good way to start out. It's low stakes, harmless, and guaranteed to get a reaction. Dad jokes are made up of silly word plays, puns, rhymes, and mildly humorous (or groan-worthy) one liners. The shorter the better!

- To tell a funny story, you need to deliver it in a psychologically satisfying way. First introduce the characters and lay a baselines context, introduce a problem or a change, set them off on a "journey," describe a climax, then have them return. Most stories fail because there isn't enough context and background established.
- Funny analogies ala John Oliver are a great way to be creative and unexpected. You could think of a topic or theme, then think of two expected items on the list before throwing in a third, unexpected item that shatters expectations. Or you could play with contrast by comparing two very different things that are nevertheless similar in a funny way.
- Misdirection is about deliberately leading your listeners down the wrong path so you can heighten the sense of surprise when you suddenly change tack.
- Finally, one way to start adding color to your stories is to be as specific as possible. Use unexpected and colorful vocabulary, imagery, and descriptions in place of boring and ordinary phrasing.

CHAPTER 3. HUMOR—IT'S A GAME

- If humor is a function of releasing psychological tension (according to the first theory of humor), then you can make a game of deliberately raising that tension (arousal) so that you can release it again for comedic effect. The greater the tension to start off with, the funnier your audience will find the joke once that tension is released.

- Create confusion, tension, awkwardness, or uncertainty and then make it obvious that you are joking. Be careful that you are "punching up" and never "punching down" or making already-marginalized groups the butt of the joke.

- You can also play with arousal by using exaggeration. Show an over-the-top or disproportionate emotion to an everyday situation to increase intensity and create a sense of "false importance." Irony can serve the same function.

- Play with social norms and expectations by using contrasts and comparisons. The surprise of contrasting two very different things can be pretty funny.

- Self-deprecation is basically making yourself the butt of a joke. You still need to use some other technique for adding in humor, though, or else you're just being mean to yourself! Self-deprecation works best when it's actually from a position or relative power or confidence.

CHAPTER 4. WALKING THE TIGHTROPE

- While it's perfectly legitimate to laugh at another's expense, it's a fine line to walk. Teasing should always be done in a spirit of playfulness—if people aren't laughing, it's not funny. Use irony, exaggeration, and funny similes to playfully insult people; it's better to target small things than attack their character in a more serious way.
- *Schadenfreude* describes the humor that comes from relishing someone else's misfortune. It can be a powerful tactic to use in small doses. Use it with people you know well or hypothetical or imaginary people, and only laugh at

things that are accidents or misfortunes rather than innate characteristics, as well as things that are relatively transient.

- Acknowledging the elephant in the room is a great way to create intimacy and familiarity. Notice what is going on that people feel unable to address directly and make a joke about it. It's important that this bluntness and candor genuinely release tension rather than increase it.
- "Benign" violations of social norms and expectations can be very funny, but tread carefully. You need to balance the pain and the relief equally.
- Deliberately misunderstanding someone or misconstruing the situation can be a funny and lighthearted way to poke fun.

CHAPTER 5. FUNNY=SEXY

- Good comedy has a lot in common with flirting. To be funnier, keep in mind that humor is a collaborative, emergent, shared phenomenon that you can't control too closely.

- Reactionary humor is an easy and effective way to get the laughs—simply exaggerate and amplify your response to something in the environment, perhaps even playing with contrast or irony.

- Invite others to join you in "banter chains" so you can create a great flow together. It's all about listening for "ins" and then changing the conversation course by introducing something exaggerated, strange, or unexpected . . . then seeing if the other person takes the bait.

- Callbacks are essentially references to previous jokes, but only work when the original joke was interesting or funny. Be patient and wait for your listeners to truly forget about it before reintroducing it.

- Catchphrases are like callbacks. Avoid cultural references and stick to making catchphrases of things *other* people have said.

- Finally, act outs are a way to bring life and dynamism to your storytelling. Use voice, gesture, expression, and nonverbal communication to convey your story with color and humor.